TOUGH Grace

in Difficult Places

A Study of the Book of Titus

From the Bible-Teaching Ministry of

CHARLES R. SWINDOLL

INSIGHT FOR LIVING

TOUGH GRACE IN DIFFICULT PLACES
A Study of the Book of Titus
Bible Companion

From the Bible-Teaching Ministry of Charles R. Swindoll

Charles R. Swindoll has devoted his life to the clear, practical teaching and application of God's Word and His grace. A pastor at heart, Chuck has served as senior pastor to congregations in Texas, Massachusetts, and California. He currently pastors Stonebriar Community Church in Frisco, Texas, but Chuck's listening audience extends far beyond a local church body. As a leading program in Christian broadcasting, *Insight for Living* airs in major Christian radio markets around the world, reaching people groups in languages they can understand. Chuck's extensive writing ministry has also served the body of Christ worldwide and his leadership as president and now chancellor of Dallas Theological Seminary has helped prepare and equip a new generation for ministry. Chuck and Cynthia, his partner in life and ministry, have four grown children and ten grandchildren.

Based upon the original outlines, charts, and transcripts of Charles R. Swindoll's sermons, the Bible Companion text was written by Brian Goins, Th.M., Dallas Theological Seminary.

Copyright © 2007 by Charles R. Swindoll, Inc.

Original sermons, outlines, charts, and transcripts:
Copyright ℗ © 2006 by Charles R. Swindoll, Inc.

All rights reserved worldwide under international copyright conventions. No portion of this Bible Companion may be reproduced, stored in a retrieval system, or transmitted in any form or by any means — electronic, mechanical, photocopy, recording, or any other — except for brief quotations in printed reviews, without the prior written permission of the publisher. Inquiries should be addressed to Insight for Living, Rights and Permissions, Post Office Box 251007, Plano, Texas, 75025-1007. The Rights and Permissions Department can also be reached at www.insight.org/permissions.

Published By:
IFL Publishing House
A Division of Insight for Living
Post Office Box 251007
Plano, Texas 75025-1007

Editor in Chief: Cynthia Swindoll, President, Insight for Living
Executive Vice President: Wayne Stiles, Th.M., D.Min., Dallas Theological Seminary
Theological Editors: Derrick G. Jeter, Th.M., Dallas Theological Seminary
  Michael J. Svigel, Th.M., Ph.D., Dallas Theological Seminary
Content Editor: Amy L. Snedaker, B.A., English, Rhodes College
Copy Editors: Jim Craft, M.A., English, Mississippi College
  Melanie Munnell, M.A., Humanities, The University of Texas at Dallas
Project Supervisor, Creative Ministries: Cari Harris, B.A., Journalism, Grand Canyon University
Project Coordinator, Communications: Dusty Rose, B.S., Communications, Dallas Baptist University
Proofreader: Joni Halpin, B.S., Accountancy, Miami University
Cover Design: Kari Pratt, B.A., Commercial Art, Southwestern Oklahoma State University
Production Artist: Nancy Gustine, B.F.A., Advertising Art, University of North Texas
Cover Image: Ingmar Wesemann

Unless otherwise identified, Scripture quotations are from the *New American Standard Bible*® (NASB). Copyright © 1960, 1962, 1963, 1968, 1971, 1972, 1973, 1975, 1977, 1995 by The Lockman Foundation, La Habra, California. All rights reserved. Used by permission. (www.Lockman.org)

Quotations marked (MSG) are from *The Message*. Copyright © 1993, 1994, 1995, 1996, 2000, 2001, 2002 by Eugene H. Peterson. All rights reserved. Used by permission of NavPress Publishing Group.

Quotations marked (NIV) are taken from the *Holy Bible, New International Version*®. *NIV*®. Copyright © 1973, 1978, 1984 by International Bible Society. All rights reserved. Used by permission of Zondervan.

Quotations marked (NLT) are taken from the *Holy Bible, New Living Translation*. Copyright © 1996, 2004. All rights reserved. Used by permission of Tyndale House Publishers, Inc., Wheaton, IL 60189 USA.

An effort has been made to locate sources and obtain permission where necessary for the quotations used in this Bible Companion. In the event of any unintentional omission, a modification will gladly be incorporated in future printings.

ISBN: 978-1-57972-790-1
Printed in the United States of America

TABLE OF CONTENTS

A Letter from Chuck

Let me ask you a question: If you had your choice, would you minister in a location covered by snow six months out of the year, with temperatures hovering in the teens, or on a sun-drenched island covered in bright-white sand and surrounded by crystal-blue water, with temperatures in the seventies year-round? If you're like me, you'd be happy to "suffer for Christ" while dozing under palm trees on a warm, sandy beach and sipping a cool drink with an umbrella in it. Sounds idyllic, doesn't it? But before you pack your Bermuda shorts and suntan lotion, you might want to leaf through your Bible to a few pages you may not have visited lately.

Buried in the back of your Bible sits a short letter penned to a young pastor, Titus, on the Mediterranean island of Crete. Rarely read and seldom quoted, this letter paints a picture of a different kind of island ministry. Crete wasn't Maui! Nowhere do we read about waves lapping or evenings at luaus. Instead, we read timeless wisdom about how to minister under difficult circumstances, regardless of where we minister.

Whether you teach your own children, lead a small group, need to evaluate the qualifications of a leader, or shepherd a flock of people, all believers are called by God to build into the lives of others. And because we find ourselves ministering in tough circumstances at times, the book of Titus should be required reading for all of us. My hope is that each lesson in this Bible Companion will help you apply God's wisdom in whatever setting He has placed you—even if it's on an island like Crete . . . or Maui!

Chuck Swindoll

Charles R. Swindoll

HOW TO USE THIS
BIBLE COMPANION

We should never confuse the unknown with the unimportant. Somewhere in the lesser-traveled pages of the Bible sits a small, three-chapter letter from Paul to Titus. Written to a young pastor on an island rife with moral relativism and religious ritualism, the book of Titus speaks to us across the centuries. In it we discover timeless wisdom about how to minister under difficult circumstances, regardless of where we minister.

Whether you choose to complete this study individually or as part of a group, a brief introduction to the overall structure of each lesson will help you get the most out of these lessons.

LESSON ORGANIZATION

 THE HEART OF THE MATTER highlights the main idea of each lesson for rapid orientation. The lesson itself is then composed of two main teaching sections of insight and application:

 DISCOVERING THE WAY explores the principles of Scripture through observation and interpretation of the Bible passages and drawing out practical principles for life. Parallel passages and additional questions supplement the main Scriptures for a more in-depth study.

 STARTING YOUR JOURNEY focuses on application to help you put into practice the principles of the lesson in ways that fit your personality, gifts, and level of spiritual maturity.

Using the Bible Companion

Tough Grace in Difficult Places: A Study of the Book of Titus Bible Companion is designed with individual study in mind, but it may be adapted for group study. If you choose to use this Bible Companion in a group setting, please keep in mind that many of the lessons ask personal, probing questions, seeking to elicit answers that reveal an individual's true character and challenge the reader to change. Therefore, the answers to some of the questions in this Bible Companion may be potentially embarrassing if they are shared in a group setting. Care, therefore, should be taken by the group leader to prepare the group for the sensitive nature of these studies, to forgo certain questions if they appear to be too personal, and to remain perceptive to the mood and dynamics of the group if questions or answers become uncomfortable.

Whether you use this Bible Companion in groups or individually, we recommend the following method:

Prayer—Begin each lesson with prayer, asking God to teach you through His Word and to open your heart to the self-discovery afforded by the questions and text of the lesson.

Scripture—Have your Bible handy. We recommend the New American Standard Bible or another literal translation, rather than a paraphrase. As you progress through each lesson, you'll be prompted to read relevant sections of Scripture and answer questions related to the topic. You will also want to look up Scripture passages noted in parentheses.

Questions—As you encounter the questions, approach them wisely and creatively. Not every question will be applicable to each person all the time. Use the questions as general guides in your thinking rather than rigid forms to complete. If there are things you just don't understand or that you want to explore further, be sure to jot down your thoughts or questions.

SPECIAL BIBLE COMPANION FEATURES

Throughout the chapters, you'll find several special features designed to add insight or depth to your study. Use these features to enhance your study and deepen your knowledge of Scripture, history, and theology.

GETTING TO THE ROOT

While our English versions of the Scriptures are reliable, studying the original languages can often bring to light nuances of the text that are sometimes missed in translation. This feature explores the meaning of the underlying Greek word in a particular passage, providing parallel examples to illuminate the meaning of the inspired biblical text.

DIGGING DEEPER

Various passages in Scripture touch on deeper theological questions or confront modern worldviews and philosophies that conflict with a biblical worldview. This feature will help you gain deeper insight into specific theological issues related to the biblical text.

DOORWAY TO HISTORY

Sometimes the chronological gap that separates us from the original author and readers clouds our understanding of a passage of Scripture. This feature takes you back in time to explore the surrounding history, culture, and customs of the world in which Titus was written.

TOUGH Grace
in Difficult
Places

A Study of the Book of Titus

A LITTLE LETTER OF ENORMOUS IMPORTANCE

Selected Scriptures from Titus

THE HEART OF THE MATTER

Buried in the back of your New Testament, somewhere between the underlined pages of Romans and Hebrews, sits a little-known and even lesser-read book. But *unknown* does not mean *unimportant*. Titus teaches us how to balance grace and godliness in three areas of our lives, creating a winning combination that draws others to Jesus Christ.

DISCOVERING THE WAY

On April 7, 1865, in the final days of the American Civil War, President Abraham Lincoln sent a nineteen-word telegram to the field general, Ulysses S. Grant. It read:

> Gen. Sheridan says "If the thing is pressed I think that Lee will surrender." Let the *thing* be pressed.
> A. LINCOLN[1]

Grant received that brief but important message and carried out the order. Two days later the bloodiest war in the history of America ended. With great dignity and humble sadness, the Confederate general Robert E. Lee donned his best gray uniform, tied a red sash around his waist, and rode his horse to Appomattox where he surrendered his armies to Ulysses S. Grant, thus officially ending the war. Nobody can say the importance of Lincoln's message to Grant could be measured by its size.

If you were to travel back eighteen centuries from that time, you would discover another enormously important message in a small and insignificant-looking package—a little letter to a man named Titus.

What do you know about the book of Titus? Can you think of a verse you have memorized or any truths from the book? What are your hopes or goals for yourself as you undertake this study?

_____

_____

_____

_____

_____

_____

As you go through the lessons in this study, why not make a commitment to read the letter weekly until you finish the study? Making your own repeated footfalls on this less-traveled road will help Titus mean more to you than just a short name.

Four Key Questions about Titus

Before we dive into the contents of the book, let's answer four key questions: Who wrote the letter? Who was Titus? Where was Titus? And why did Paul write to Titus?

Who wrote the letter? The author left little to guess with the first word—_Paul_ (Titus 1:1). Picture him as a 60-year-old, seasoned missionary. At that time of his life, he was an itinerant evangelist, a faithful pastor, a founder of churches, a servant of God, and an apostle of Christ. Far from retirement, Paul actively engaged in eternal things and mentored younger men who would extend ministry far beyond him. Yet he knew that he was nearing the end of his life and wanted to create a legacy of faith for the generations to come.

As you can see from the map below, Paul moved intentionally and deliberately after being under house arrest in Rome from AD 60–62.

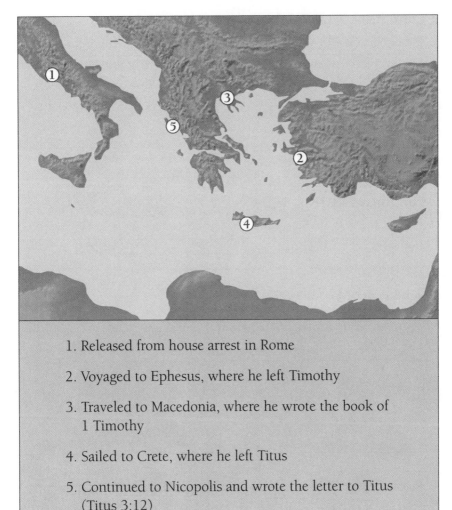

1. Released from house arrest in Rome

2. Voyaged to Ephesus, where he left Timothy

3. Traveled to Macedonia, where he wrote the book of 1 Timothy

4. Sailed to Crete, where he left Titus

5. Continued to Nicopolis and wrote the letter to Titus (Titus 3:12)

Who was Titus? We do not know how Paul and Titus met, but we do know Titus was thoroughly pagan when they first crossed paths. Born to Gentile parents, Titus met the seasoned missionary and became Paul's "true child in a common faith" (Titus 1:4)—that is, his disciple in a close mentoring relationship.

What do the following passages tell you about Titus? Try to use brief descriptive words or phrases to characterize him.

2 Corinthians 2:13; 7:6, 13–14

_____

_____

2 Corinthians 8:16–17, 23

_____

_____

2 Corinthians 12:18

_____

_____

Galatians 2:1–3

_____

_____

Titus 1:4

_____

_____

We know Titus journeyed with Paul to the booming metropolis of Corinth. It was there in the "sin city" of their day that Titus watched Paul minister, handle problems, and grow a church. As they ministered together, Titus became the poster child of grace—_grace_, the unearned, undeserved favor of God. When the apostle Paul traveled to Jerusalem carrying the message of grace, he took with him uncircumcised Titus, a man transformed by the gospel and unfettered by legalism, the belief that God's favor could be gained by works. Titus knew that conforming to the Mosaic Law, the religious rules of the Jews of his day, did not add to or validate the righteousness of Christ (Galatians 2:3–5).

God wasted nothing in Titus's life. Titus was reared in a pagan home . . . mentored by Paul . . . given an internship at a bustling, problem-filled church . . . endowed with an appreciation of grace . . . and affirmed before church leaders in Jerusalem. With every step, God was preparing this young man to stand alone as His spokesperson to a culture rife with paganism and to churches contaminated by error.

Where was Titus? Titus was on the Greek island of Crete (Titus 1:5). Many of us may consider this a dream of "island ministry"—cool breezes and sandy beaches. But this island was a far cry from a vacation. There was much to be done. As Paul's ship slipped into the blue Mediterranean, Titus stood there in his sandals and waved good-bye to his mentor for the last time. Then, with his heart pounding in his throat, he turned back to what would become his realm of ministry.

 DOORWAY TO HISTORY
On Assignment in Crete

Crete was an island long past its prime and inhabited by people with questionable lifestyles. After its status declined around the time of the birth of Christ, Crete became a breeding ground for mercenary soldiers and shifty traders.[2] Paul chose one of their own poets to describe the character of the island dwellers: "Cretans are always liars, evil beasts, lazy gluttons" (Titus 1:12).

Paul's concern for this wayward island may have been sparked when he landed there briefly on his way to Rome (Acts 27). He witnessed an island filled with transients, an island confounded by an amalgamation of religious beliefs—in short, an island desperate for life-changing grace.

The crass culture of Crete had seeped through the church walls (Titus 1:10). The church had become tainted by greedy legalists and saturated with selfish gluttons. In his letter to young pastor Titus, Paul's instructions were clear:

- Rebellious voices must be silenced! (1:11)

- Let no one disregard you! (2:15)

- Warn those who are unruly twice, and then have nothing to do with them! (3:10)

Instead of relaxing in the Mediterranean sun, Titus had to prepare himself for the spiritual challenges of the Cretan society!

In what ways does your culture resemble the one in Titus's day? Can you see ways in which the culture today is negatively affecting your church? Be specific.

_____

_____

_____

_____

Surely Titus had fear and doubt in his heart: "Can I do it? Am I up to the task? What if I fail?" What are some fears you have about ministering to people within your specific culture or group as you face its specific challenges?

_____

_____

_____

_____

Is there a particular ministry opportunity that God has nudged you toward that you have run from because of fear? If so, what was it you were afraid of?

_____

_____

_____

Why write Titus? Paul stated his purpose in Titus 1:5: "That you would set in order what remains and appoint elders in every city as I directed you." When Peter preached the first sermon on Pentecost, people from Crete were in the crowd (Acts 2:11). Some chose to believe in Christ and returned to the island to establish churches. One problem persisted, however: these new believers were not rooted in sound doctrine or grounded in solid biblical faith.

Titus was left to stand alone for truth in a society of immature believers, strong and stubborn legalists, passive and lazy island dwellers, false teachers who stood against the truth and would stand against him, and those who taught truth but lived a lie. Paul wrote this little letter as a great encouragement for his protégé. He gave him a game plan for growing congregations in a callous culture.

If you were Paul writing an encouraging letter to someone taking on a new leadership role in your church or in your current arena of ministry, knowing the culture, how would you encourage him or her? Be specific.

_____

_____

_____

_____

_____

SURVEYING THE BIG PICTURE

Titus found himself in the midst of a transient culture with fleeting values. Sound a bit like today? In a culture of frequent moves, caffeine-powered schedules, and a constantly spinning moral compass, how do we help people grow to become more like Christ? In the case of Titus, Paul showed him the way by weaving a fabric of two main threads—blending grace with godly living. In fact, he did that in every chapter of the book of Titus:

- Chapter 1—Balancing grace and godliness in the church

- Chapter 2—Balancing grace and godliness in the home and family

- Chapter 3—Balancing grace and godliness in the world

If Christians will live out this message of Titus, we will find evangelism far easier. When we live a life that stands on grace and is based on grace, those without Christ are drawn to us. When believers blend sound doctrine with true godliness, we have a message that cannot be ignored. We strive to be rooted in God's grace and God's mercy and God's power and, at the same time, we evidence that we live differently from the world's system. We think differently, we act differently, and we respond differently.

STARTING YOUR JOURNEY
Many Christians may score high on biblical knowledge but struggle with application. Others may model godly living but leave doctrine for those "more theologically minded." As we walk through this letter to Paul's protégé Titus, we will discover why both grace and godliness are crucial to every area of our lives. Specifically, we will discover three lingering lessons.

First, *grace and godliness make a church effective and stable.* When a congregation embodies a message of grace and godliness, it snuffs out legalism and repels false teaching. The church begins to speak more about what God has done for the church than what the church must do for God. Such freedom in grace helps the church become effective and stable.

Second, *grace and godliness make a home sensible and sane.* Over and over again in this letter we will read the word *sensible.* Chapter 2 of Titus will teach us how grace and godliness can help us unlearn negative habits and mind-sets that many of us grew up with. For a great number of people in our world and even in our churches, "home" is not an oasis or sanctuary from trouble. The front door opens more often to stress and anxiety than to sensibility and sanity. Grace can bring order out of chaos, and godliness will calm the commotion.

Third, *grace and godliness cause the world to be curious and attracted.* If the church is doing what God desires it to be doing, it will be the most winsome, magnetic place in the community. People will prefer being there to being anywhere else except their homes. If the congregation models grace and godliness in the community, people outside the church walls will find a way in.

Of the three principles, which one seems to jump out at you most today? Which area of grace and godliness needs honing in your life?

Before delving into the next lesson, take time to read each chapter of Titus. Under the following headings, write down your observations of how the text relates to each lesson, and note how this applies to your own circumstances.

Chapter 1—Grace and Godliness Make a Church Effective and Stable

_____

_____

_____

Chapter 2—Grace and Godliness Make a Home Sensible and Sane

_____

_____

_____

Chapter 3—Grace and Godliness Cause the World to Be Curious and Attracted

_____

_____

_____

❧

Like Lincoln's short note to Grant, Titus is a small letter steeped in significance. In it we will discover that grace and godliness are not optional but essential to the Christian life. As you work through the lessons of this Bible Companion, we hope you will unearth treasures for a life of grace and godliness that have been buried in your Bible for centuries.

TWO MEN ON A MISSION, WITH US

Titus 1:1-4

THE HEART OF THE MATTER

Paul and Titus ministered side-by-side until the apostle dispatched his young protégé for a difficult task in a difficult place. Knowing that Titus had nobody to bolster his faith when he felt low or encourage him when he was criticized, Paul wrote a short but significant letter to fill that need. Though they were separated by many miles, both men shared the same cause. And though we live two thousand years later, we, too, are called to live out our identity in Christ and fulfill our personal calling to make disciples of Christ.

DISCOVERING THE WAY

Most communication today comes by way of electronic mail. Let's face it; it's fast, it's easy, it's relatively simple. With small ticks of your index finger you can transfer it, forward it, save it, or delete it. Yet there's something about a handwritten letter that touches our hearts. Whether it's the unique penmanship, the slash of a pen, an ink-smear, or the embossed stationery, handwritten notes reveal a special relationship between the sender and receiver. As we have seen, Paul identified himself at the beginning of the letter. Titus must have cherished this scroll not only for its content but because it reminded him of his dear friend.

If you were to use five words or titles that paint a picture of your identity as an individual, what would they be?

_____

_____

_____

Are the words you chose descriptive or action-oriented? What might this suggest about how you view yourself?

_____

_____

_____

Paul, the Writer

In the first three verses of Titus, we learn three key characteristics about Paul: his identity, his purpose, and his calling.

 Read Titus 1:1

Doctors write "MD" after their names. Scholars append "PhD" to theirs. And authors list their books in a bibliography. In our world, credentials matter. The apostle Paul, too, had credentials:

- Jewish Pharisee educated under the renowned scholar Gamaliel

- Roman citizen with training in Greek literature and philosophy

- Founder of multiple churches and possessor of supernatural spiritual gifts

But he didn't list his accomplishments when he identified himself in his letter to Titus.

According to Titus 1:1, how did Paul identify himself?

_____

_____

With whom was Paul's individual identity linked?

_____

What do you think Paul was trying to communicate to Titus about his own self-identity?

_____

_____

Paul humbly called himself a "bond-servant," but he was also an "apostle of Jesus Christ." An apostle was a special messenger with a special message sent on a special mission. The apostle recognized that his authority came not from his background or his message but from the One who sent him—Jesus Christ Himself. As Titus organized churches, appointed elders, and went toe-to-toe with the legalists who sought God's favor through good works, he did so with the authority of an apostle supporting him. He must have curled up near the candle with this scroll many a night and read it over and over and over again.

Though God would use Paul to write almost half the books of the New Testament, Paul humbly called himself the servant and messenger of One far greater than he.

 Read Titus 1:1–3

In just two lines we hear Paul's life purpose or, more aptly, his creed. Paul saw his first role as leading people to the Lord Jesus Christ. Second, Paul equipped them with the "knowledge of the truth" (Titus 1:1). *Disciples* of Christ motivated Paul more than simply *decisions* for Christ. He recognized that making disciples took time, effort, and intentionality. Third, Paul encouraged new believers through their every struggle, extending to them the hope of eternal life (1:2).

He accomplished this high purpose by responding to a high calling—the preaching of God's Word (1:3).

 DOORWAY TO HISTORY
Proclaiming the Message

Before e-mail, the telephone, the telegraph, or even a postal service, messages still needed to get out. If a public official or king had an announcement for his subjects, he would call a herald to proclaim the message or, in Greek, the *kerygma*.

Much like a "town crier" in the Middle Ages, this man would travel from village to village, gather the people, and "proclaim the word" from the king. The verb form, *kerysso*, means "to declare an event."[1] Paul embraced his purpose of proclaiming the saving events of Christ's life when he wrote to the church at Corinth: "And when I came to you, brethren, I did not come with superiority of speech or of wisdom, proclaiming to you the testimony of God" (1 Corinthians 2:1). In his last letter, he passed on his calling to Timothy, "Preach [or proclaim] the word" (2 Timothy 4:2).

If somebody were to ask you to tell him or her your purpose or goal in life, how would you answer? It might take some time, especially if you haven't thought about it before, but go ahead and try your hand at drafting your purpose statement below.

_____

_____

_____

How does this purpose fit with the picture you painted of your personal identity earlier in this lesson?

_____

_____

_____

Paul's response to Christ's calling to proclaim God's message fed a spiritually famished culture. Similarly, our own world needs the same heralds. Fed on a steady diet of cotton-candy theology and me-focused sermons, even many of our churches enjoy the taste of God's Word without any nutritional benefit. People in our postmodern world are starving for truth.

In just a few words we discover the mission that kept Paul up at night. Confident in his identity, clear on his purpose, and committed to his calling, Paul commissioned his young protégé to embark on a similar journey.

Read Galatians 1:11–16. Describe Paul's past.

_____

_____

_____

How long ago had God determined Paul's purpose? When Paul learned of his purpose, how did this affect the actions he took toward his future?

_____

_____

_____

Titus, the Recipient

As Titus unrolled the scroll and saw the familiar name of his beloved mentor and friend, Paul, his mind must have traveled back over well-worn paths: long evenings bantering by the campfire with Paul, enduring trying circumstances together, experiencing the lowest moments and celebrating the highest. To Titus, that tiny letter must have been cherished as a moving memorial of a friendship he would never forget.

What friends and mentors in your past have helped you establish your identity as a Christian and set you on your present course of life and ministry? How did they do this?

_____

_____

_____

_____

_____

_____

_____

 Read Titus 1:4.

In this short verse we discover significant depth. Paul revealed his personal bond with Titus, noted their common faith, and bestowed a divine blessing before continuing with the purpose of his letter.

To Titus, Paul was more than merely a friend and mentor. He was family. Though Paul led countless people to Christ and called many people his co-laborers, partners, and colleagues, there were precious few he called "my true child" (Titus 1:4).

Though Titus was a fully grown man, capable of leading and orga-nizing churches on a spiritually barren landscape, Paul still viewed

Titus as his "child." Paul helped "birth" Titus into a new reality. Then Paul acted as his spiritual father. He helped him take his first steps in the Spirit, grow on the milk and meat of the Word, and mature into a man of God. Yet, Paul never pulled rank.

Notice how Paul followed his endearing term with the phrase, "in a common faith" (1:4). As a mentor Paul built *into* Titus, but as a Christian Paul built *together* with Titus for the cause of Christ. They shared the same status before God. Titus embraced the same grace that transformed Paul. Paul walked with the same Spirit that indwelled Titus. Relationally Titus would always look up to Paul, but spiritually they stood on the same ground under the shadow of the same cross and in service of the same Lord.

Paul spoke of his personal bond with Titus, reminding him of their common faith, then reiterating a divine blessing: "Grace and peace from God the Father and Christ Jesus our Savior" (1:4). Grace is the unmerited favor of God. Peace is reconciliation with God and others. Paul wanted to ensure Titus never overlooked or ignored these precious truths.

It was fitting that as Titus embarked on a difficult mission without his dear mentor, Paul wanted to bless him with grace and peace. It was as if Paul were saying, "Titus, remember God's grace. Grace to you. God's unmerited, unsolicited favor, may it pour on you. May it mark your life. May it characterize your ministry in this graceless land. And when the dark night fills your soul, remember God's peace. May that peace envelop you at night after tilling the soil of hardened hearts. May you know a peace that passes all understanding."

STARTING YOUR JOURNEY

Paul's words encouraged Titus as he embarked on a vital mission. Now, nearly two thousand years later, we are on the same one—to carry on the Great Commission by making disciples wherever the Lord leads us (Matthew 28:19–20). Paul's scroll may have been addressed to his young protégé, but in a way, he wrote it for us. Paul lived his magnificent life and then died. Titus fulfilled his calling, and he, too, died. We are here today to read and heed the same message Paul sent Titus. From his example we can glean a few important lessons we can apply to our lives.

First, *Paul explained his identity using two monikers, "servant" and "apostle"* (Titus 1:1). In this way he summarized the essential aspects of his identity.

Read Ephesians 1:1–12 and list the words or phrases that describe the identity of a believer in Christ.

_____

_____

_____

_____

As you compare these words or titles with the five words you used at the beginning of this lesson, what changes, if any, would need to take place for you to more fully live out your identity in Christ?

_____

_____

_____

_____

Second, *Paul's purpose in life revolved around three specifics that served as reference points on his life map: bringing people to faith in God, leading them to knowledge of the truth, and giving them hope of eternal life.*

What elements make up your goal in life or the purpose statement you wrote earlier? What few things will guide you when the
world pulls you in disparate directions?

_____

_____

_____

_____

Third, *Paul knew his calling and carried it out.* He knew God created
him to preach the Word without apology in whatever circumstance he
found himself.

**Read Matthew 28:19–20. What is our mission as believers in
Christ?**

_____

_____

_____

_____

Paul's call to be a foreign missionary may not be yours, but your
own life purpose should somehow fit into Christ's command to
"make disciples." As you think of the various ways to do that,
what kinds of activities motivate you?

_____

_____

_____

_____

Finally, *Paul modeled what a deep spiritual relationship looks like.* Though they were not related by blood, he and Titus had a deep familial bond that only comes through a committed relationship of mentoring.

With whom are you cultivating a deep and intimate relationship? Do you have a true son or daughter in the faith? Are you a son or daughter in the faith to somebody else? Write their names here:

_____

_____

_____

_____

If you don't yet have these kinds of important relationships, pray that God would bring them into your life, then contact individuals who might fill this disciple-making need in your spiritual life.

The questions in this lesson are not necessarily meant to be answered immediately, nor are they intended to make you feel guilty. God gave us biblical models for our personal reflection. Give yourself permission to dwell on these questions. Take time in prayer and meditation this week to ponder these issues and answer the questions as honestly as you can. They may help you return to a purpose and a calling that have been buried under temporary and fleeting cares.

LOOKING FOR A FEW GOOD MEN
Titus 1:5–9

THE HEART OF THE MATTER

Few things are more important for a local church than having the right people in leadership. Many of us have experienced the fallout from poor leaders: mismanagement of people, disharmony, disunity, erosion of purpose, and poor and unwise decisions, to name just a few. So it's no surprise to read that, immediately after his introductory greeting to Titus, Paul stressed the necessity of finding qualified elders or overseers. Before ministry work can even start, the right men must be found. And to find them, we need to know what we are looking for.

DISCOVERING THE WAY

"The worst moment was when we realized the pilot had no idea what to do next." So writes British author and pastor Tom Wright about a time when he and other passengers were flying over South Africa in a malfunctioning plane. "We might not have realized how serious the situation was," Wright continues, "if the pilot had not . . . handed the map back to us with an air of desperation. 'Well,' he said, 'you see if you can figure out where we are!'"[1]

Wright and his party made it safely to their destination, but he ends with this wise observation. "When the pilot can't figure out what's going on, the whole plane is in trouble."[2]

What happened in that airplane can happen in a church. A person not spiritually qualified to lead has no business piloting the lives of others. Unfortunately, we often don't find out how disqualified the person is until we're helpless to do anything about it.

This brings us to a six-word principle that should never be forgotten—it is woven through the fabric of the verses we'll examine in this lesson: *Good spiritual leadership requires being qualified.* It isn't enough just to be zealous or concerned for those who don't know Christ. It isn't enough just to have some gifts or training or education. A spiritual leader must possess certain character qualities, blended with a measure of maturity, or that leader has no business leading a church. Good spiritual leadership requires proven qualifications.

How do you think good business or social leadership compares with good spiritual leadership? If the choice were up to you, what characteristics would you look for to determine whether someone is qualified for spiritual leadership?

_____

_____

_____

The Main Reason Titus Was Left

As Paul's ship slipped into the blue waters toward Nicopolis, two things were on his heart as he waved good-bye to Titus. First, his work was left unfinished, and second, qualified leaders remained to be chosen. These tasks Paul left to his friend and partner, Titus.

 Read Titus 1:5.

Titus's first responsibility was to "set in order what remains" (Titus 1:5). If you had metal in your mouth during those awkward teenage years or have broken your leg, you understand what the verb phrase "set in order" means. It's the Greek word *epidiortho*[3], from the root word *ortho*[4], which is where we derive our words *orthodontics* and *orthopedics*. Just as braces set teeth in order and a cast straightens a broken limb, so Titus was assigned to "make straight" the churches in Crete that had been fractured by theological debates and splintered by moral ineptness.

Paul did not recommend that Titus accomplish this daunting task by himself; he knew that setting things in order requires a team. So Paul followed his first command with a second: "Appoint elders in every city as I directed you" (1:5). An elder was a leader, someone who would help Titus accomplish this task.

On an island 160 miles long containing several cities, Titus needed a crack team of spiritually qualified leaders to fix deep fractures caused by gossipers, rebels, deceivers, and hypocrites (1:10). Paul told Titus to "silence" them (1:11). It was a tough assignment. Not only that, but Titus would be dealing cross-culturally with "those of the circumcision"—Jews—while Titus himself was a Greek. People must be dealt with carefully, not attacked. All of this would take wisdom, tact, and planning. That is why Titus needed the help of a few qualified overseers.

Describe the worst church experience you've ever had.

_____

_____

_____

_____

_____

Chances are good that a part of the problem was rooted in poor leadership. How would you rate the leadership involved in your experience?

_____

_____

_____

The "Blameless" Qualities Elders Must Possess

Finding a qualified team is easier said than done. Poor leaders abound—you can find one around almost every corner. But locating qualified leaders, the ones with backbones of steel to withstand the pressure of rebellion, gossip, and hypocrisy—well, that is like looking for the proverbial needle in the haystack. What was Titus to look for in selecting elders or overseers?

Paul instructed Titus to look into three critical areas of a leader's life. And in each one the elder must be "above reproach" (Titus 1:6). Note that the leader must be blameless, not sinless. If a leader has skin, he has sin! Perfection is not required, but unquestioned integrity is.

 Read Titus 1:6–8.

First, the potential elder must be blameless in his marriage and family. To find qualified leaders, the place to begin is behind the front doors of their houses.

The elder was to be a "one-woman man," as it reads in the Greek (1:6). By this qualification, Paul indicated that the positions of church elders are to be filled by men—specifically by men who are married. Different interpretations flourish, and perhaps single men could be considered for the position of elder, but it's safe, at the very least, to say the command applies to men who are married, widowers, or widowers who have been remarried. Most importantly, the qualification highlights the faithfulness and sexual purity a man models with his wife.

Not only was he to be the "husband of one wife," an elder must have "children who believe" and who can't be "accused of [wasting their lives in] rebellion" (1:6). As with the phrase above, it's hard not to approach this stipulation with countless questions and contingencies. What about the man with a wild child? Is the elder off the hook when his child moves out of the house? In this text, the word used for "children" means those living under the authority of the elder, not a general reference to adult children.[5] The apostle encouraged Titus to take stock of the whole home and not just one child who may decide, out of his or her own free will, to follow a wayward path.

Second, an elder must not only be blameless in his home, he must be blameless in his heart—in his character and conduct (1:7–8).

As though it were a preflight checklist, Paul gave eleven qualifications that one should review before taking off with a leader. Five are negative (1:7), and six are positive (1:8). Taken together, these characteristics form the composite identification of a proven spiritual leader.

An elder must not be "self-willed." That is, he must not be self-pleasing—consumed with his own opinions and absorbed with his own interests. He must not be one who is "quick-tempered," which means one who is prone to anger, who nurses an angry spirit, or who seethes with anger under the surface like molten lava flows under a volcano. Nor should a spiritual leader be "addicted to wine." The idea here is of a person who lives with a beer bottle in his hand, not one who has a drink occasionally. A leader must never be "pugnacious," always itching for a fight. God requires leaders to lead his sheep, not drive, assault, or attack them. Finally, an elder must not be "fond of sordid gain" or one who preys on vulnerable people to benefit financially. There are many who seek prosperity under the guise of ministry, but blameless leaders never do.

On the positive side, leaders are to be "hospitable, loving what is good, sensible, just, devout, [and] self-controlled" (1:8).

Sound demanding? God doesn't mess around when it comes to the spiritual growth of His people. We are too valuable to Him. Whether for good or evil, an elder wields enormous influence on a church.

Read Titus 1:9.

As Paul closed his instructions to Titus on how to spot qualified elders, he revealed how they should operate when people are watching. These leaders are not prized for their power of persuasion, their creativity in the boardroom, or their business acumen, but for having "a good grip on the Message, knowing how to use the truth to either spur people on in knowledge or stop them in their tracks if they oppose it" (Titus 1:9 MSG).

When turbulence shakes the congregation, these leaders hold on firmly to the Bible. They cling to it and embrace it as a matter of life and death. It's their source of information and the filter for how they make decisions. And they use it to help those they lead become spiritually mature.

Looking back at the example you gave earlier of a negative church experience, which of the qualifications of a godly elder were violated or ignored in that situation?

_____

_____

_____

What were the consequences (for you, for the church body, for the community)? Why do you think God takes the choosing of spiritual leaders so seriously?

_____

_____

_____

_____

_____

How seriously do you take the instructions for evaluating and choosing spiritual leaders that we've studied from Titus 1?

Not Very		Somewhat		Very
1	2	3	4	5

God takes these qualifications seriously. Why did you evaluate your level of seriousness as you did?

_____

_____

_____

STARTING YOUR JOURNEY

Many of our churches today are like airplanes flying with unqualified leaders. Just as it's dangerous to our physical safety to fly with an unskilled pilot, it's dangerous to our spiritual safety to follow a weak or tragically flawed elder. To ensure your safety, look for these credentials in your spiritual "pilot."

First, *in the privacy of the home, the spiritual leader earns the right to be respected.* Look behind closed doors and drapes. Look into the lives of the other people in the home. If a man is respected by those who know him the best, he is respectable.

Consider the elder you know the most about or the one whose ministry role touches your life most directly, perhaps your pastor (no names, please). With the goal of evaluating leaders according to biblical standards, how would you characterize this person's marriage?

_____

_____

_____

How is his relationship with his children?

_____

_____

_____

Second, *in his personal life, the spiritual leader models the reasons to be selected.* If you were to evaluate your pastor or elders against Paul's criteria, how would they fare? Look carefully into the details of the leader's life. Is he a man of integrity? Is there godly consistency in his character? If so, you have a spiritual leader worth selecting.

On the graph below, shade in the degree to which you think these eleven traits apply as a life pattern to the person you evaluated above. (Keep in mind as you complete this evaluation that the goal is not to be critical or to provide a reason to gossip, but to apply biblical mandates to those in roles of spiritual leadership.)

Always					
Sometimes					
Never					
	Self-willed	Quick-tempered	Addicted to Wine	Fighter	Greedy

Always					
Sometimes					
Never					
	Hospitable	Loving/Good	Sensible	Just	Devout	Self-controlled

Finally, *in the public arena, the spiritual leader protects others.*
Whether it's in the church or in the community, a spiritual leader
tends to the hurting, protects the preyed upon, and rights wrongs. He
carries a shepherd's crook both to guide and to protect the sheep.

**Reread Titus 1:9. Look up "exhort" and "refute" in a dictionary.
How well do your leaders do in exhorting you to grow spiritually?**

_____

_____

_____

**How well do your leaders do in protecting you from those who
would deny the truth of the Bible?**

_____

_____

_____

**Look back over your evaluations, both negative and positive. If
you have a say in selecting leaders for your church, will these
evaluations influence your decisions? Why, or why not?**

_____

_____

_____

⁂

Remember our six-word principle: *Good spiritual leadership requires
being qualified.* Titus could never "set things in order" without the
help of proven leaders. Just as it's dangerous to discover a pilot's lack
of qualifications *after* you are in the air, churches need proven and
trusted elders before they embark upon new ministries.

DEALING WITH THE DIFFICULT AND DANGEROUS
Titus 1:10-16

THE HEART OF THE MATTER
Living in the real world presents harsh realities we cannot escape and dare not ignore. People often think the evil empire is limited to the frightening underworld of terror-ists and gangsters, rapists and molesters, thieves and murderers. The truth is, there are enemies who appear righteous but are equally as evil. The Bible calls them false teachers—those who look holy but teach lies. Being masters of deceit, they prey on the unsuspecting and the naive using spiritual tactics and silky speech often laced with Bible verses. Unless they are identified, refuted, and silenced, their evil influence will take a serious toll on the body of Christ. As it did in Titus's day, standing firm for truth demands discernment, courage, and integrity.

DISCOVERING THE WAY
It would be convenient if fences could stave off false teachers, but unfortunately, the enemy imbeds them sub-tly into our congregations. Satan is highly intelligent and wickedly insidious, awaiting any opportunity to trap or deceive. It was up to Titus to find elders who would care for their congregations with a high commitment to the truth of Scripture and the gut-level courage to confront those who oppose it, because wherever the truth is being proclaimed, it will also be attacked.

In your opinion, how truthful are we as a culture? What evidence do you see of this trend?

_____

_____

_____

THREE WRONGS FALSE TEACHERS COMMIT

Jesus said, "Beware of the false prophets, who come to you in sheep's clothing, but inwardly are ravenous wolves" (Matthew 7:15). Elders must be ready to fend off wolves that would prey upon the flock. So Paul exhorted Titus to keep a wary eye for three signs of danger: false prophets' words, their motives, and their actions.

 Read Titus 1:10–11.

False teachers say the wrong things—that's why they are false. Paul called them "empty talkers" (Titus 1:10). Their words sound true, they speak with conviction, but they twist the truth into lies.

These wolves are "rebellious" (1:10), insubordinate, a "law to themselves" (Romans 2:14)—they eschew accountability from godly leaders and reject the authority of Scripture. Yet they speak eloquently, beautifully, and appear spiritual. They lure the unsuspecting and untrained with smooth speech and conjured-up credentials. Rooted in rebellion, these teachers sprout forth hollow words and bear the fruit of deception. Once others digest their morsels, "whole families" will be upset (Titus 1:11).

The New Testament is full of warnings about false teachers. What do you learn from each of the following verses about how to identify a false teacher?

1 Timothy 1:3–7

_____

_____

1 Timothy 6:3–10

_____

_____

2 Timothy 2:14–16

_____

_____

2 Peter 2:1–9

_____

_____

1 John 2:21–24

_____

_____

Jude 8–16

_____

_____

Do you know of any false teachers in your church or in society in general? Who are they, and what do they teach?

Paul didn't mince words when he told Titus they "must be silenced" (Titus 1:11). False teachers must be muzzled. And this command, to silence false teachers, doesn't apply only to pastors but to all who lead in the church, at any level. Our responsibility is to muzzle liars and deceivers. As shepherds, whether we lead a small group or a large congregation, part of our job of caring is to courageously confront evil. But to do so, we must know the truth. C. S. Lewis wrote, "If all the world were Christian, it might not matter if all the world were uneducated. But . . . to be ignorant and simple now—not to be able to meet the enemies on their own ground—would be to throw down our weapons."[1]

On a scale of one to five, how well do you feel you know the truths of Scripture? (How confident are you in your ability to pinpoint spiritual or theological untruths when you encounter them?)

Not Very Well		So-So		Very Well
1	2	3	4	5

Besides working through this Bible Companion, what else are you doing to keep sharp your knowledge of biblical truth?

Read Titus 1:11–13.

False teachers not only say the wrong things, they also have wrong motives. They love to prowl near the fainthearted, hoping to hide their wrong motives behind smooth words so they can devour the unsuspecting.

Two motives quickly surface in these verses. First, false teachers place an overemphasis on size, numbers, and comparative growth. They have an intense interest in building a large following. Second, behind their silky and flowery language is the passion to line their own pockets. Their greed motivates them to attract a large crowd. Paul used the term "sordid gain" (Titus 1:11). Eugene Peterson's *The Message* renders this phrase as "all for the sake of a fast buck." Inevitably their teaching motivates people to shower the "teacher" with tangible tokens of gratitude. They use their position for financial profit.

Paul warned Timothy of this when he said,

> If anyone advocates a different doctrine and does not agree with sound words, those of our Lord Jesus Christ, and with the doctrine conforming to godliness, he is conceited and understands nothing; but he has a morbid interest in controversial questions and disputes about words, out of which arise envy, strife, abusive language, evil suspicions, and constant friction between men of depraved mind and deprived of the truth, who suppose that godliness is a means of gain. (1 Timothy 6:3–5)

Peter also warned believers in his churches to be wary of false teachers. Read 1 Peter 5:2–4. In contrast to false teachers, what attitudes should characterize good spiritual leaders?

_____

_____

_____

Paul told Titus false teachers can be spotted by their wrong motives and also by their absence of character. Paul, widely read and knowledgeable of his audience, quoted a Cretan philosopher to prove this point. "Cretans are always liars, evil beasts, lazy gluttons" (Titus 1:12). Paul didn't dispute this characterization; it was "true" (1:13). They were liars, lawless, lazy, and lustful.

A hidden motive of greed mixed with an absence of character is a volatile recipe for destruction. So false teachers' mouths must be muzzled and their practices rebuked (1:13). The integrity of the truth and the protection of the church are too important to allow them to continue to mix their poison. But Paul also had the false teachers' welfare in mind. Correction was meant to motivate them to "sound . . . faith" (1:13).

 Read Titus 1:14–16.

False teachers' wrong words and hidden motives eventually are manifested with wrong deeds. They pay too much attention to myths and man-made commands (Titus 1:14); they embrace a twisted understanding of purity (1:15); and they say they know God but their actions deny Him (1:16). The supreme indictment against false teachers is they "turn away from the truth" (1:14).

Besides listening closely to teachers' words, questioning their motives, and looking at their actions, how else can you determine if what they present is true? Based on the work of John R. W. Stott, here are three questions to ask.

First, what is the *origin* of the content, God or man? Can you find this "truth" in the Scriptures, based on careful interpretation? Or has it been derived from human philosophy?

Second, what is the *essence* of the message — its distilled truth? Does the message emphasize and encourage a Christian's spiritual life or only the pleasures and rewards of the physical life?

Third, what is the *result* if you heed the teaching? Will you become more like Christ? Or will you become merely "spiritual," following ritual "do's and don'ts" of the latest spiritual fad?[2]

Remember, truth is divine in its origin, spiritual in its emphasis, and transforming in its effect.

Consider this scenario. You are part of a weekly Bible study or small group. One of the members is struggling to make ends meet financially. The leader of your group advises her to "name it and claim it," assuring her that all she needs to do is truly believe that God's favor is upon her and that He really wants her to be wealthy and her problem will be solved. How would you go about assessing whether this is wise, godly counsel?

Would you say anything to the Bible-study member? To the leader? If so, what would you say? What should be your motive?

STARTING YOUR JOURNEY

If you're one of Christ's sheep, you're probably a shepherd. You don't carry a crook and wear sandals, but you lead sheep. Unconvinced? Do you serve in a church? Do you teach a children's Sunday school or lead a Bible study? Have you taught your kids about Christ? Have you introduced someone to Christ? If you answered yes to these or similar questions, you're a shepherd. And just like a shepherd you must nourish and care for the sheep, as well as protect and defend them. So you must be wary of wolves. To do that, here are three principles God honors.

First, *commit to living in the real world*. God never promised life would get better. In fact, in many ways it has gotten worse. We need to wake up and face reality squarely, with discernment.

Read 1 Chronicles 12:32. What made the "sons of Issachar" stand out in this list of names? Could you be considered a son or daughter of Issachar? Why, or why not?

_____

_____

_____

Look up the word *discernment* in a dictionary, and write its definition in your own words.

_____

_____

_____

What does Philippians 1:9–10 indicate is the result of this quality? How does one receive it? (See also 2 Chronicles 1:7–10 and James 1:5.)

Second, *carry on a courageous strategy.* When it comes to truth, we live in a placidly passive world. Anything offered up as truth is accepted as truth, usually without question. But calling wrong right can have devastating results, so men and women must have courage to confront that which is not biblical truth.

Go back and reread Titus 1:11, 13. What is Paul's two-pronged strategy for confronting false teachers? What contemporary methods can you think of to put Paul's message into effect?

According to Titus 1:13, what is the purpose of confrontation?

When we are fearful to stand up for God, what does He command and promise in Joshua 1:6–7, 9?

Finally, *hold the standard high*. If you are in a position of leadership, never settle for just getting by, and never allow people to shirk the standards. Hold on to the truth of the Bible. Never allow it to be compromised or customized to fit someone else's idea of truth.

In what areas of your life do you find yourself slipping away from God's standard?

_____

_____

_____

How does this affect your integrity and your right or ability to speak up for biblical truth?

_____

_____

_____

What will you do this week to shore up your commitment to living, speaking, thinking about, and standing for the truth?

_____

_____

_____

❦

Confronting false teachers isn't fun; it is always difficult. Regardless of the difficulty, though, it's necessary if we are to grow in our faith and enable others to grow in theirs. Chances are good that at some point you'll be faced with the dilemma of speaking up or shutting up. Speak up! With discernment, courage, and integrity, you just might pull a poor lamb from the mouth of a vicious wolf.

OLDER MEN AND WOMEN: LISTEN UP!

Titus 2:1-4

THE HEART OF THE MATTER

For years, Christians have likened the church to a family. Not to a slick, efficient business full of professionals; not to a theater for actors, directors, and stage hands; and not to an academic institution, where intellectually gifted faculty members teach courses and students earn degrees. No, the church is God's earthly family, where brothers and sisters grow up together, laugh and play together, suffer and hurt together, and especially where we learn to get along, encourage, and even correct and admonish one another so that the family might remain close and committed. In the second chapter of Titus, Paul gave Titus some helpful and much needed "family counsel"—counsel that will challenge us to age gracefully as well as to honor those who are older than we are.

DISCOVERING THE WAY

People are watching you. Like it or not, our lives are almost always on display. Even when we don't realize it, people record their observations and form opinions. The saying in television is, "The camera is always on." Whether on the set or in our homes, someone is watching. And that is nothing new.

Even as far back as Jesus's day, He taught His disciples:

> You're here to be light, bringing out the God-colors in
> the world. God is not a secret to be kept. We're going
> public with this, as public as a city on a hill. If I make
> you light-bearers, you don't think I'm going to hide
> you under a bucket, do you? I'm putting you on a
> light stand. Now that I've put you there on a hilltop,
> on a light stand—shine! (Matthew 5:14–15 MSG)

There it is—you're being watched, like a candle flickering in the darkness.

**Just as others are watching you, you are watching others—
whether you realize it or not. Whose "light" do you find yourself
noticing and watching? What "God-colors" does that person
bring out in the world?**

_____

_____

CATEGORIES OF PEOPLE SINGLED OUT

People have always watched how God's people live their lives. Paul
wanted, therefore, to put the churches in Crete on the alert to this
fact. He began with their pastor, telling Titus—*You're being watched*
(Titus 2:1). Then he told the men and women, both older and
younger—*You're being watched* (2:2–8). And to believing slaves he
said, *Even you are being watched* (2:9–10). Some good advice for all of
them and for us as well is to pay careful attention to our character and
to our faith (1 Timothy 4:16), for surely others are.

THREE WHO ARE INITIALLY IDENTIFIED

Whether we live in a city, on a farm, or on a small island like Crete,
which is 160 miles long and 40 miles wide, people form opinions
about our lifestyles. After Paul addressed Titus, he delivered wise
words to older men and then to older women.

Read Titus 2:1.

Paul opened chapter 2 with two small but significant words: "But . . . you. . . ." As though pointing a finger at Titus's sternum, Paul addressed the leader before he talked about the people. He exhorted Titus to "speak the things which are fitting for sound doctrine" (Titus 2:1). This doesn't apply only to preaching but to conversation as well. All speech, public and private, needs to be wholesome, healthy, and nourishing. Our words should be "sound," from which we get our word *hygiene*.[1] Healthy words lead to a healthy, wholesome lifestyle. Paul said it starts with those who teach or lead people because they're under a magnifying glass. That's why James 3:1 says, "Let not many of you become teachers, my brethren, knowing that as such we will incur a stricter judgment." People take notes on leaders' lives. They remember whether or not their speech matches their steps.

What does Proverbs 12:18 say about our words? What word pictures does Solomon use to describe the effects of our words? What are the implications?

_____

_____

_____

Do you know someone who "speaks rashly"? What is your estimation of that individual?

_____

_____

_____

What would you guess his or her age to be?

_____

Do you know someone who speaks wisely? What is your estimation of that individual?

_____

_____

_____

What would you guess his or her age to be?

_____

Generally, older people are wiser, more mature, and stronger in their faith. But not always. Job's words are a splash of cold water on the face: "The experts have no corner on wisdom; getting old doesn't guarantee good sense" (Job 32:9 MSG). However, older, wiser, godly saints are a treasure to the body of Christ. They bring stability and strength, vigor and vitality.

Skim through the following passages, noting the individual's age and describing his or her attitude.

Genesis 17:15–21

_____

_____

Genesis 18:9–15

_____

_____

Genesis 21:1–7

_____

_____

Joshua 14:6–15

_____

_____

GETTING TO THE ROOT
What Does "Older" Mean?

How old is "older"? The Greek word *presbutes*, translated as "older" in Titus 2:2, "an old man" in Luke 1:18, and "aged" in Philemon 9, appears only three times in the New Testament. Paul used it of himself in Philemon, and we know from his chronology that he was probably 60 years old when he wrote that letter. The word is used in Luke to describe Zacharias, whose wife, Elizabeth, was "advanced in years," or past the childbearing years. Non-biblical sources use the word to refer to men as young as 50. So we can conclude that when Paul said, "older men," it applies to men who are 50 and older.[2]

Read Titus 2:2.

Older, righteous men are described in Psalm 92:12–14 as fruitful palm trees and fragrant cedars. "They will still yield fruit in old age; / They shall be full of sap and very green" (92:14). Still flexible, still supple, still learning, still growing—this picture of aging isn't what most people see. Sometimes men can become more stubborn and less teachable as they age; they develop an unyielding disposition that calcifies into a critical spirit. That need not occur! Paul says they can and should do just the opposite!

What should be the marks of an older godly man, according to Paul?

First, he should be *temperate*, not extravagant and over-indulgent. The word *temperate* is often used for being free from intoxication or any form of addiction.

Second, he should be *dignified*, or respectable and honorable. He should not be frivolous, superficial, or trivial.

Third, he should be *sensible*, possessing good judgment, discernment, and common sense. He should know when he is saying too much or not enough. The immature find themselves enslaved by their passions; godly older men have learned how to control their impulses.

The first three marks reveal respectability earned over time; the final three portray consistent maturity as years go by. As you look at the next three characteristics, you discover the word "sound" appears before "faith, love, and perseverance." Again, it's our word for "hygiene." An older man is characterized by health in all three of these areas.

Fourth, he should be *sound in faith*. Having lived for 50, 60, or 70 years, an older man should know that God can be trusted. He has stories of God's faithfulness; he's a great comfort to younger men weighed down by anxiety and insecurity.

Fifth, he should be *sound in love*. This is *agape*, or unconditional love. Such men seek the highest good for their fellow men and women. They love without expectation and without conditions.

Sixth, he should be *sound in perseverance*. The picture is of someone who can hold up under the load. He does not try to escape the pain or throw off his responsibility. He trusts the Lord through adversity, knowing it will make him stronger in the long run.

Older men of this caliber are rare but invaluable to the body of Christ. They serve as living advertisements for how to age with grace.

Think of some older Christian men you know. Have they become more spiritually vibrant or less? Why?

_____

_____

_____

Older men who possess the six characteristics listed by Paul are a wealth of wisdom and blessing. Which of these have you seen displayed in men you know or have known? Write the name of the person next to the trait.

Temperate _____

Dignified _____

Sensible _____

Sound in faith _____

Sound in love _____

Sound in perseverance _____

Circle those traits which seem to you to be the most rare in older men. Why do you think this is so?

_____

_____

_____

Consider those men you know who exhibit some or all of these traits. If you had an opportunity to honor them with words, what would you say?

Dear _____,

_____

_____

_____

_____

_____

Why don't you write such a note and mail it this week?

Read Titus 2:3–4.

Turning his attention to older women, with the same word he used for older gentlemen, Paul applies a similar command. Just as older men were to live lives of holiness, "Older women likewise are to be reverent in their behavior" (Titus 2:3). They are to demonstrate godliness. These women should point others to the things of God; they should model His message authentically. Additionally, Paul said, they shouldn't have reputations as "malicious gossips" or be "enslaved to much wine." Older women should be known as those who guard their lips from saying things about others that are demeaning, slanderous, or hurtful. And they are to diligently avoid addictions. Instead, they should be known for their godliness and temperance.

Furthermore, Paul exhorted the women to teach "what is good" (2:3). Not only do older women teach their children, but their lives serve as models to younger women. If you are an older woman, remember, you're being watched. Younger women may not clamor for your attention, but they are closely watching your actions. Paul moved from "teach" in verse 3 to "encourage" in verse 4. He recognized that younger women need encouragement, and who better to offer it than women who have been in their shoes! Paul encouraged older women to intentionally build into the lives of younger women.

Using the criteria Paul outlined, do you know a godly older woman? What have you learned from her?

_____

_____

_____

_____

If you had an opportunity to honor her with words, what would you say?

Dear _____,

_____

_____

_____

_____

_____

Why don't you write such a note and mail it this week?

STARTING YOUR JOURNEY
The camera of younger eyes is always on, watching how those who are older handle tough circumstances, juggle responsibilities, and maintain their testimony in a coarsening culture. The church family is desperately in need of those who model faithful, godly living. Their value cannot be underestimated!

Age mixed with maturity provides a credibility that cannot be ignored. Those who have matured in sound faith, love, and perseverance possess a credibility not easily disregarded. They don't have to ask for it or carry a résumé. They don't have to brag or tell people about their accomplishments. Their life history and seasoned walk with God make them worthy of honor and respect.

Read Leviticus 19:32. Write in your own words how we are to treat "the aged." How do our actions toward them relate to God?

_____

_____

_____

Modeling and mentoring cultivate an integrity that won't be forgotten.
Perhaps you have had one or a few mentors in your life. You can
probably quote their words that made an impact on you without your
realizing it at the time. You remember their godly heritage, and it left
a permanent record in the archive of your mind.

**What are the three most important lessons you learned from
people who have acted as mentors in your life?**

1. _____

2. _____

3. _____

**When was the last time you thanked God for your mentors? They
were not placed in your life by accident. Write a prayer of thanks
for them below.**

_____

_____

_____

_____

_____

Older men, older women—listen up! You're being watched. Younger
men, younger women . . . as you watch your elders, honor them.
Paul's message was loud and clear. In order to safeguard the unity
of the church family and pass along the faith to succeeding generations, older men and women must model the traits listed in Titus 2.
Whether we're older or younger, let's remember to live holy lives, for
we are all being watched by the world.

LESSON SIX

MAKING YOUR TESTIMONY
SLAM-DUNK CONVINCING

Titus 2:4–10

THE HEART OF THE MATTER

It seems as though Christians are always searching for ways to share the gospel. We want the person we're talking with to understand the importance of knowing Christ personally and to be convinced that Christ can truly revolutionize his or her life. Of all the methods available for sharing the gospel, there is one that is not only effective, it's impossible to ignore or deliberately push aside: living an authentic Christian life. Living in accordance with what we believe is what holds the secret of convincing others that Jesus Christ has transformed our lives—and that He can do the same for them. And it all starts in our close relationships. If we can't love and respect those closest to us, how will we love and respect strangers?

DISCOVERING THE WAY

As we discovered in our last chapter, people are watching us. The camera is always rolling. That doesn't mean we need to be picture-perfect or sinless. We just need to say more often those words that tend to get lodged in our windpipes, "I'm sorry. I was wrong. Please forgive me." And that's never more needed than in our close relationships. The book of Titus gives us guidelines for living a Christlike life in our home and work environments.

In this lesson, we'll focus on what those actions should be. In lesson eight, we will focus on how authentic Christian living influences the rest of the world.

REMINDER OF THE CONTEXT OF TITUS 2

When people *see* us living authentic Christian lives, they will be more open to *hear* spiritual things from us. Paul didn't send Titus a letter full of theories. He encouraged a blend of theory and practicality: the truth of the gospel with proof from a changed life. As we saw in the first three verses of Titus 2, Paul sent his message of genuine Christianity first to Titus (2:1) and then to older men (2:2) and older women (2:3), telling them all to teach and to model godly living.

Cultivating a life of authenticity requires life interacting with life—older men and women impacting those younger. Unfortunately, in our transient and generationally fragmented culture, this doesn't happen all that often. Many people have replaced personal guidance from accessible people with impersonal advice from inaccessible people, such as afternoon talk-show hosts and celebrities.

Who have been your mentors? What is one thing you learned from watching their relationships with those closest to them?

Mentor	Lessons Learned

THREE GROUPS WHOSE LIVES ARE BEING WATCHED

Because people are watching to see if our actions line up with our beliefs, in this next section of Scripture Paul addressed two more groups: the younger men and women, and the employed. How we conduct ourselves within these realms will influence how others view the God we serve.

 Read Titus 2:4–5.

Paul addressed the women first. It was never Titus's responsibility—nor any male pastor's for that matter—to mentor younger women. That was the job of the older, wiser women, who would "preach" with their lives. They were to come alongside younger women and "encourage" them (Titus 2:4).

Now, before we look at the details of what kind of encouragement younger women should receive, we must keep in mind that these specifics don't apply to every woman's situation. Paul particularly had in mind young women who were married and starting a family.

Older women were to affirm these younger women "to love their husbands [and] . . . their children" (2:4). Older women should demonstrate a "sensible," reverent, or self-controlled life. From them, younger women can learn how to be faithful to their husbands. Seasoned grandmothers can teach new mothers how to remain kind under the strain of working in the home. And they can set an example of what it means to submit to their husbands (2:5).

Paul's advice runs counter to the message of today. What images are women asked to live up to in our culture in contrast to Paul's instructions?

_____

_____

_____

_____

In what seven areas does Titus 2:4–5 instruct younger women?

1. _____

2. _____

3. _____

4. _____

5. _____

6. _____

7. _____

If you are a woman, place a check mark next to each quality you feel you generally model. For those you don't, place an "X." (For those that are not applicable, place "N/A.") How can you be who God made you to be, with your unique personality, and still be obedient to these seven commands?

_____

_____

_____

Many women bristle under the notion of submission to their husbands, but as John Stott affirms, "'subjection' contains no notion of inferiority and no demand for obedience, but rather a recognition that, within the equal value of the sexes, God has established a created order which includes a masculine 'headship' . . . of responsibility and loving care."[1]

Read Titus 2:5 again, paying special attention to the end of the verse. What should be a young woman's motivation for submitting or being "subject" to her husband? What message about Christianity might it send others if she doesn't?

Godly homes open a door for the gospel. People rarely see couples who model both sacrifice and submission. And when they do, they want to know how to reproduce it under their own roofs because it paves the way for harmony and peace in a marriage. Looking for a place to have a ministry? Start right at home. It may be the hardest job you'll ever do, but the benefits for the cause of the gospel are immense.

 Read Titus 2:6–8.

Paul then turned Titus's attention to the young men in the congregation. He urged Titus to slow down the young stallions. Just as he cautioned the young women, he said young men were "Likewise . . . to be sensible" (Titus 2:6). They were to control their tongues and their tempers, bridle their ambition appropriately, and put a stop to their greed. Titus was to help them corral their sexual urges and impulses so they wouldn't be driven by their glands rather than their minds.

How was Titus to get his message across? He was to model it. The young men needed a *tupos*, or "example." [2] The Greek word was used for stamping or making an impression into a coin or wax. Titus was to stamp his life upon the young men of Crete. Paul's instructions also apply to men today. As they model these qualities, their close relationships will flourish.

In what four areas does Titus 2:7–8 instruct young men?

1. _____

2. _____

3. _____

4. _____

If you are a man, place a check mark next to each quality you feel you generally model. For those you don't, place an "X." How do you think your spouse or friends would characterize your reputation in these areas?

_____

_____

What is the result, according to Titus 2:8, of authentically living out these characteristics?

_____

_____

_____

 Read Titus 2:9–10.

These verses concern Christian slaves, but we can apply Paul's principles to employer-employee relationships. Without making commentary on the institution itself, Paul laid out instructions that apply to any of us who have a boss or who make our living in the workplace.

Paul highlighted two areas that will make or break how we portray our Christian faith at work—diligence (Titus 2:9) and character (2:10). Christians, more than anyone, should accomplish what is expected with a great attitude. We are to "be subject . . . in everything" without being "argumentative" (2:9). Nothing cuts away at the morale of an organization like employees who harbor a negative spirit about the boss they work for, the people they work with, or the kind of work they do. Whether manifested by gossip at the watercooler, rudeness, or shoddy craftsmanship, how we accomplish the tasks before us reflects upon the God we serve.

Secondly, Paul moved from accomplishing diligent work to maintaining a consistent *character*. We are not to pilfer (2:10). *Pilfering* refers to theft, whether petty or grand. When we realize people form opinions of Christ based upon our actions or inactions, office supplies won't find their way into our briefcases, time on-the-clock won't be flippantly wasted, expense accounts won't be padded, and embezzlements won't happen on our watch.

Instead of stealing, what does this passage say employees should do?

_____

_____

What is the result of diligent work performed by one who possesses Christian character, according to Titus 2:10? (Hint: Try looking up this verse in various translations.)

_____

_____

_____

STARTING YOUR JOURNEY
Do a quick inspection: What do your attitudes and actions say about the Christian life?

Paul admonished us to "adorn the doctrine of God" (Titus 2:10). Paul's use of *kosmeo*, "adorn," means to "decorate" so as to "do credit to" the gospel,[3] just as an expert craftsman deliberately arranges jewels on broaches, necklaces, or crowns to show off their beauty.

Having a well-lived, authentic Christian testimony is like setting the jewel of the gospel in such a way as to make the truth appealing, attractive, and lovely. Merely observing you may never bring someone to a saving knowledge of Christ, but your actions (and inactions) can draw attention and make others wonder about what makes your life so attractive. You show people who Jesus is before you ever say a word. *The most effective presentation of the gospel begins with a Christlike life.*

On a scale of 1 to 5, how well do the following areas of your life showcase the jewel of the gospel?

	Gospel Is Unattractive/ Hidden		Gospel Is Dull and Cloudy		Gospel Is Alluring/ Brilliant
Home Life	1	2	3	4	5
Work Life	1	2	3	4	5

Read Titus 2:4–10 again. What specific actions or inactions contribute to the results you noted above? What can you do to enhance the way you showcase your faith in your relationships at home and at work?

_____

_____

_____

_____

If someone were to ask you why your life is different, what would you say? How would you explain the influence of your faith on your actions?

_____

_____

_____

_____

There's something very convincing about an authentic Christian life lived consistently day-to-day. Authenticity was so important to Paul that he reminded us three times of the impact of our lives on furthering the gospel. Because we are on public display, we should not dishonor the Word of God (Titus 2:5) but shame the opponents of the gospel (2:8) and adorn God's truth (2:10). If we are to tell others about Christ, we must first show them Christ in our close relationships. Only then will our testimonies be "slam-dunk" convincing.

TOUGH GRACE
Titus 2:11–15

THE HEART OF THE MATTER
There are few doctrinal truths more important, more
valuable, and more misrepresented than grace. While
many embrace it and live it, thanking God for liberating
them from sin's authority, others abuse it by reveling in their sin "so
that grace may increase" (Romans 6:1). Just as love must be tough
when some would take unfair advantage of it, so it is with grace. True
grace—tough grace—sustains God's high standard of obedience,
which results in a life marked by self-control and godliness.

DISCOVERING THE WAY
Unlike other trees whose foliage drops to the ground in
the fall, leaving the tree to stand naked through the long
winter, the live oak's leaves cling to its branches through
the cold months. Stubbornly, the brown leaves withstand wind, snow,
and ice until the sap warms again. Only in spring, when new life
surges through the tree's branches, will the dead leaves finally lose
their grip.

Just as new life breaks the grip of an oak tree's dead leaves, so
coming to grips with God's grace will loosen our natural love for sin.
This is not easily done because we stubbornly cling to old passions,
believing God's grace is a license to continue to sin. That's cheap
grace. Thankfully, Paul taught "tough grace": when we truly embrace
God's grace, we won't abuse it but will delight in obedience.

What's wonderful about these final verses in Titus 2 is that they present what grace *includes*—not an exposé on all of the abuses of grace but rather a series of theological statements explaining how grace impacts our spiritual lives. Then, in the middle, a statement about "tough grace" emerges in bold relief.

Try to summarize in one sentence what you already know about grace.

_____

_____

_____

GRACE AND SALVATION

In describing a grace relationship with God, Paul began at the beginning—the salvation of souls.

 Read Titus 2:11.

The Greek word translated as "appear" is *epiphany*. It refers to "a visible manifestation of a hidden divinity, either in the form of a personal appearance, or by some deed of power by which its presence is made known." [1] It pictures a hero, often a god, such as Apollo, breaking into a helpless situation to rescue someone from danger or peril. Paul declared that the hero is "grace," implying the person and work of Jesus Christ, who broke into the world and destroyed the power of sin over humanity. Salvation pictures a holy God coming near to unholy man for no other reason than to bestow His unmerited favor.

Who are the recipients of God's grace? Paul said, "all people" (Titus 2:11 NLT). So, was he advocating universal salvation? Not at all. When Jesus bore the sins of humanity on the cross, He opened the door of hope; He made liberation *possible* to all who are willing to receive it.

Read John 14:6. What did Jesus say about Himself? How is one saved?

_____

_____

_____

Read John 1:12. What do you have to do to become a child of God? Who is the "Him" in the verse?

_____

_____

_____

Romans 3:22–25 describes God's act of mercy, in which He declares believing sinners righteous while they are still in their sinning state (this is called *justification*). That doesn't mean that God *makes* us righteous so that we never sin again; rather, He *declares* us righteous—much like a judge pardons a guilty criminal. Because Jesus took our sin upon Himself and suffered our judgment on the cross, God forgives our debt and proclaims us PARDONED.

In order to take part in this gift, we must step forward into the relationship with God that He has prepared for us—not by doing good works or being a good person but by coming to Christ just as we are and accepting His justification and redemption by faith.

Have you received justification and redemption through Christ by believing in Him through faith? If you haven't or are unsure, please read "How to Begin a Relationship with God" at the back of this Bible Companion.

GRACE AND SANCTIFICATION

Grace delivers us from sin's clutches, freeing us from the eternal *penalty of sin*. But we are still hounded by the temporal *power of sin*.

Read Titus 2:12.

In Titus 2:11, Paul described grace as a saving hero. Then in verse 12 he told Titus that it's a teacher. Grace teaches two lessons. One is negative, and the other is positive. First, it instructs us to learn to say no to "ungodliness and worldly desires" (2:12). Second, it teaches us to say yes to a life pleasing to Christ — "to live sensibly, righteously and godly in the present age" (2:12).

The purpose of these two lessons is our sanctification — to grow us up in Christ, to make us more like Him, and to set us apart for God's purpose. Grace, though tenderly saving us, is a tough teacher instructing us to "straighten up"! Why? Because we can. Before we trusted Christ we had no power to say no to sin's grip. But once we have placed our faith in Jesus and experienced His forgiveness, we can say yes to God and be loosed from sin's dominion.

 DIGGING DEEPER
Sanctification and the Holy Spirit
The doctrine of sanctification is central to the Christian life. The word "sanctify," *hagiazo*, has the same meaning as "holy" — to set something apart for a sacred purpose.[2] All Christians are set apart from sin and made a part of God's family at the moment they believe in Christ (John 1:12–13; 1 Corinthians 6:11). But there is also a progressive sanctification whereby we are made more like Christ in our daily lives (1 Peter 1:16). Ultimately, when we reach heaven, we'll be completely set apart from sin to holiness, a state which is sometimes called glorification (Ephesians 5:26–27). *Sanctification, then, is the setting apart of Christians to holy living, which is accomplished through a progressive work of the Holy Spirit within humans to make us more like Christ, culminating in completion in heaven.*

Though God the Father and Jesus are involved in a Christian's sanctification, it's the Holy Spirit working with us to free us from sin's power and making us like Christ. Specifically, the Spirit's power woos us to love God (Romans 5:5), enables us to reject sin (Romans 8:13), transforms us into Christ's image (2 Corinthians 3:18), and provides Christlike character (Galatians 5:22–23).

Do you ever feel you are destined to continue committing the same old sins? Until we are with Christ in heaven we'll stumble and fall, but the Bible provides wonderful instruction that can help us overcome sin. For example, what do Galatians 5:16 and 2 Corinthians 3:17–18 tell us?

_____

_____

_____

_____

Paul used the metaphor of an instructor to teach the doctrine of sanctification in Titus 2:12. In Romans 6:17–23 Paul used another metaphor: "slave." What does Paul say about a believer's slave status?

In the past we were slaves of _____.

In the present we are slaves of _____.

But just because we are now "slaves to righteousness" doesn't mean we always choose to live that way. Unfortunately, we often choose to return to our old master, sin. Would your behavior today brand you as more of a slave of righteousness or of your appetites and desires? Explain.

_____

_____

_____

GRACE AND GLORIFICATION

The doctrine of salvation shows us what grace provides. Sanctification tells us what grace teaches us now. Glorification looks ahead at what grace perfects.

 Read Titus 2:13.

Paul continued his instruction on grace by reminding Titus that he had a "blessed hope." Not only did grace save him from sin and was sanctifying him to Christlikeness, but grace gave Titus great anticipation of seeing Christ return in His glory.

When Christ comes to take us to our eternal home, He will glorify us—making us like Himself, faultless—and will right all wrongs. Read the following passages and list some of blessings and wonderful experiences you can look forward to.

Ephesians 1:3–4

_____

_____

Hebrews 11:15–16

_____

_____

Revelation 21:1–5

_____

_____

_____

With this knowledge in mind, how should you live your life today? What do you need to give up? What do you need to cling to?

_____

_____

_____

GRACE AND REDEMPTION

How can God take slaves to sin and make them adopted children of heaven? How does He give wretches like us a hope for a blessed future? The answer is grace. When we accept God's grace for salvation we also accept His grace of redemption—we're bought from the bondage of sin to live in holiness.

Read Titus 2:14.

Paul made it clear to Titus that Jesus, as an act of grace, "gave Himself for us to redeem us." Through His death on the cross, Christ bought back what was His—us. He ransomed humankind from the bondage of "every lawless deed."

Though redeemed, many choose to live as if they are still sin's slave. So Paul stressed that such redeeming grace wasn't a license to continue in sin. Christ redeemed the Cretans and us, "to purify for Himself a people for His own possession, zealous for good deeds" (Titus 2:14).

How would you respond if a fellow Christian asked you, "What's the point of avoiding sin when the price has already been paid?" See Romans 6:1–2, 15.

_____

_____

_____

When we abuse grace, making it a license to sin, what are we ultimately doing, according to Jude 4?

_____

_____

_____

Memorize Ephesians 2:8–10 this week. What "good works" has God set you apart to perform? Do you think sin hinders your fulfillment of that purpose?

_____

_____

_____

STARTING YOUR JOURNEY

Like the live oak tree, as we embrace the foundational doctrines of grace, our old leaves begin to fall off. Our natural desires are replaced by the supernatural cravings for God's love, truth, and grace. No wonder Paul said to Titus at the end of Chapter 2, "These things speak and exhort and reprove with all authority. Let no one disregard you" (Titus 2:15). There are few places today where truth is still being taught with authority. Instead we hear a message of cheap grace, which says just live however you'd like, or of legalism, which reduces the Christian life to a list of do's and don'ts. But when the truth is revealed, growth occurs. A maturity develops and sheer love for the Savior pushes out the old, dead, rotten leaves to make room for divine, new ones.

Titus served on an island steeped in religiosity and carnality. Paul knew grace was the only doctrine that would break the chains of legalism and motivate people out of their complacency. Grace would not only free the Cretans from sin's power, it would force them out of their long-standing desire to keep serving the old master: sin.

What was true for Titus and his church is true for us today. When we really grasp God's grace, it should overwhelm us with such a love for Christ that we no longer want to return to our old, sinful ways. That's tough grace—when the power of our new affections overcomes the grip of old, bad habits. So what's the big deal? *When we truly embrace grace, we won't casually abuse grace.*

Read Romans 7:14–25. We face the same dilemma with sin as Paul did. Based on this passage and what you've learned in this lesson, what is the answer to your dilemma with sin? How does grace factor in to the equation?

_____

_____

_____

_____

Christ's demonstration of grace to us will never be matched. Using the letters G-R-A-C-E, what word(s) can you think of to describe how His grace helps you overcome sin's power?

G_____

R_____

A_____

C_____

E_____

The enemy would like to shame you into believing that you are characterized by your sin, but if you're a believer in Christ, you are characterized by His righteousness. What does 1 John 1:9 promise? Write a prayer of confession below, asking God to forgive your sins and to give you wisdom to embrace His grace.

_____

_____

_____

_____

_____

⚜

The dying leaves of a live oak tree will be pushed off only by the surge of new life. In the same way, when we find ourselves clinging to our old ways, we must reignite our hearts with godly affections. Paul reminded Titus of four core doctrines rooted in grace. Not the cheap grace of flippant belief and loose living but a tough grace filled with a passion to obediently follow the God who saves, sanctifies, glorifies, and redeems unworthy people like us. Whenever we start feeling the urge to cling to our old ways, we can revisit these verses in Titus. For when we do, we'll embrace new life again . . . in His grace.

LIVING BEFORE A WATCHING WORLD
Titus 3:1–8

THE HEART OF THE MATTER

There is no more exacting ordeal for a Christian than living under the scrutiny of others who are taking mental notes of our lives. Many are looking for a reason to reject Christ. Finding inconsistencies fuels their fire of unbelief. But non-Christians live only in the here-and-now and are unaware of another, better world—the eternal. How convincing it is, to a skeptical world, to be able to peer through a crack in the eternal door and see Christ in a life marked by authenticity and good deeds.

DISCOVERING THE WAY

Two very real worlds exist. The Bible teaches it and Christians believe and understand it. Much of humanity, however, is unaware of this fact and often unwilling to accept it. We're of course talking about the "seen," or temporal, world and the "unseen," eternal world. In our desire to open the eyes of the unbelieving world, believers sometimes fail to remember that our message of a powerful and loving God and of life after death may not be welcome.

Do you know people who deny or doubt the existence of eternal life? What are their reasons for doubting?

_____

_____

_____

Have you tried to open their eyes to the biblical view of eternity? If so, what did you do or say, and how successful where you?

_____

_____

_____

REMEMBERING THREE STATEMENTS FROM THE SCRIPTURES

Our world is dark, desperate, and doubting. The Lord has left believers here and hasn't taken all of us to heaven because He has chosen us to be witnesses to His mercy, grace, and love. Specifically, Christians have three callings.

- First, because the world is dark and without hope, Jesus calls us to be *light-bearers* (Matthew 5:14–16).

- Second, because the world is desperate for real affection, we are called to be *love-givers* (John 13:34–35).

- Third, because the world doubts authentic faith, we are called to be *respect-earners* (1 Thessalonians 4:9–12).

Jesus did not ask us all to be eloquent speakers or theological geniuses; He merely asked us to live out eternal values in front of people who have never seen beyond the visible world. Our authentic lives, our good deeds, and our godly behavior are what will crack open the door of eternity for people to peer through.

BEING SUBMISSIVE CITIZENS AND GOOD NEIGHBORS

Few posts were as dark, desperate, and doubting as the island of Crete. Paul knew Titus needed wisdom on how new believers could enlighten a closed culture whose minds and hearts were blinded by the glaze of relativism and ritual. And so, getting very practical, he told Titus they needed to be reminded "to be ready for every good deed."

Read Titus 3:1–2.

The first good deed that Titus was to instruct the believers in Crete to perform was to submit to the government (Titus 3:1). To most people reading this today, the command hardly seems significant or difficult. But the Roman government of the first century was nothing like most of us will ever experience. Rome was ruled by immoral, corrupt, unjust, and oppressive rulers. But Paul didn't give Titus a way out with a qualifier like, "As long as the government is fair, obey it."

We see this command elsewhere in Scripture too. What does 1 Peter 2:13–14 command us to do regarding government?

_____

_____

_____

What should be our motivation for obeying this command according to 1 Peter 2:15? What is the result of our obedience?

_____

_____

_____

Throughout Scripture, God is clear that our responsibility is to honor those He places in authority. In extremely rare cases, we may be forced to disobey that authority if the government requires us to disobey God's commands. And though civil disobedience has occurred historically, a Christian's normal behavior toward the government should be that of deference and honor.

Paul gave Titus another good deed he should remind the churches to follow—be a good neighbor. And if Titus was wondering what it meant to be a good neighbor, Paul gave him four practical ways to be neighborly (Titus 3:2).

First, Titus was to remind believers that they were not "to malign [anyone]." The Greek word for malign is where we get our word *blasphemy*.[1] The Christians in Crete were not to speak ill of their neighbors, put them down, slander them, curse them, or treat anyone with contempt.

On the positive side they were "to be peaceable." They shouldn't be contentious and belligerent in word or deed. Elsewhere Paul made it very clear: "If possible, so far as it depends on you, be at peace with all men" (Romans 12:18).

Third, the Cretan Christians should be "gentle." Because everyone is plagued with weaknesses and foibles, Paul encouraged the church to indulge some of these human frailties. They should believe the best about people and give them room to make mistakes.

Finally, they should show "every consideration for all." Especially due to their culture at the time, no greater grace could be shown the islanders than for the believers to be humbly courteous to all regardless of race, political leanings, religion, marital status, gender, and background.

Sometimes it can be easy to overlook the importance of these qualities or take them for granted. In column B below, describe the opposite characteristic or action.

A (Titus 3:2)	B
Malign no one	
Be peaceable	
Be gentle	
Show every consideration for all	

When you see someone acting out the behavior in column B, what do you assume about that person's beliefs or values? Do you tend to want to move toward or away from him or her?

_____

_____

_____

What is your typical reaction to the behavior in column A?

_____

_____

The world has come to expect Christians to act like the world, so when we model respect for the government or graciously love unlovable neighbors they begin to wonder what makes us different. Then, we've won the right to be heard.

"Christians are not perfect, just forgiven" is a common but true phrase. As you consider your actions this week, do you need to apologize to someone for an action you committed in column B? If so, write out your apology and commit to giving it soon.

_____

_____

_____

_____

Humbling Reminders and Amazing Grace

Moving from what Titus and the Cretan Christians should *do*, Paul told them *why* they should be submissive citizens and good neighbors.

 Read Titus 3:3–7.

Titus was to remind his fellow believers that they once lived on the other side of eternity. While the door was closed, they desperately groped in the dark, doubting they would ever see the light. But God's kindness "appeared" (Titus 3:4). Like a hero shattering the darkness, God saved them "not on the basis of deeds . . . done in righteousness," but out of His amazing grace (3:5).

And God's grace, by the power of the Holy Spirit, who was graciously "poured out . . . through Jesus Christ," infused life into their dead souls and gave them a new moral purpose (3:5–6). The same is true of us! As believers, we should never forget that we once lived in darkness until the light of Christ pierced our dark hearts and, by His grace, justified us. Even while we were in sin, God declared us righteous and "made [us] heirs according to the hope of eternal life" (3:7).

What five key words in the passage indicate what God did for us while we were in the darkness of disbelief?

Titus 3:4 _____

Titus 3:5 _____

Titus 3:6 _____

Titus 3:7 _____

What was your life like before you met Christ? Read Titus 3:3 again closely. With which elements of Paul's description do you most readily identify?

_____

_____

_____

_____

_____

_____

What was it that gave you that first glimpse that something existed beyond this superficial, imperfect world? How can you use this insight and your personal experience you described above to be a light-bearer to others, to show them a better, eternal world exists?

_____

_____

_____

Balancing Right Belief and Convincing Behavior

Having instructed Titus on what believers should do before a world lost in darkness and doubt, Paul summed up his command with *how* Titus should encourage believers to live in front of a watching world.

 Read Titus 3:8.

Paul told Titus to speak confidently to his congregations, telling them that living in the light will open the door of eternity for those living in darkness. He urged Titus not to shrink behind the fear of ruffling a few feathers but to be bold.

And what was Titus to say? To all "those who have believed God," he was to command them to "be careful to engage in good deeds." Paul, the apostle of grace, felt this message was so important, he mentioned the phrase "good deeds" five times in his letter to Titus (2:7, 14; 3:1, 8, 14). Doctrine (belief in and about the Lord) must work together with deeds. This is the message Titus was to give—doctrine and deeds will prop open the door to heaven so that those living in a dark, desperate, and doubting world can see Christ.

Doing good deeds with integrity goes against our human nature. How are Christians able to do the good works God desires of us?

_____

_____

_____

STARTING YOUR JOURNEY

Paul's words to Titus indicate that most Christians don't need another course on evangelism; they need reminders of how to live before a watching world. Two thousand years ago Jesus departed heaven and entered this world. He modeled how to open eyes darkened by spiritual blindness. He told the truth without apology, and He modeled the message He preached. We are to do the same. But in order for us to be light-bearers in a world of darkness, love-givers in a world of desperation, and respect-earners in a world of doubters, we must remember a couple of things.

First, *it takes authenticity and integrity to win a hearing.* When we, as believers, model integrity and are real with people, it opens their eyes. People admire Christians who admit rather than omit their struggles. We should be the first to apologize when we offend someone. Our unbelieving neighbors will not judge us if we are less than perfect and know it. Submitting to the government and treating our neighbors with kindness and respect will open doors and open minds to the message of Christ.

Read James 2:14–20 and Matthew 5:13–16. What are the results of failing to do good works? What are the benefits, especially to non-believers, of Christians doing good works?

_____

_____

_____

Second, *it's impossible to convince anyone of any truth you are not living.* Those living behind the unseen door of eternity are watching and waiting for inconsistencies. Our lives must model the message we preach with our lips. Our right beliefs must be balanced with right behavior. When we say we believe in a forgiving God, we must be willing to forgive. If we speak about marriage being a lifelong covenant but cannot show respect and love for our spouse, our neighbor begins to wonder whether faith in Christ really means anything at all.

In the table below, write what you believe about living the Christian life and then write a corresponding deed you actually practice in your life. Finally, in the last column place an "I" for "Inconsistent" or a "C" for "Consistent," to check whether your doctrine and deeds work together.

Principles of the Christian Life	Deeds	I/C

Look at all of your "I's." What do you need to do this week to begin turning these into "C's"?

_____

_____

_____

When Christians model consistency, integrity, and authenticity, others see a glimpse of whom we really are, "heirs according to the hope of eternal life" (Titus 3:7). They see that there is something more than—something beyond—this broken, worldly existence: the hope of heaven.

The Scripture is clear: "Whoever will call on the name of the Lord will be saved" (Romans 10:13). But how can they call on the name of the Lord in faith if "they have not heard? And how will they hear without a preacher? How will they preach unless they are sent?" (Romans 10:14–15). We've been sent to preach Christ with our lives to a world groping in the darkness. They are desperate for love and doubting anyone can truly live out what they believe. God calls us to carry the light of Christ to dispel the darkness by how we live our lives, because before a watching world our lives reflect the Savior—and that is a matter of life and death.

THE TOUGH SIDE OF MINISTRY

Titus 3:8-11

THE HEART OF THE MATTER

Both hospitals and churches face a similar danger—the healthy may catch a disease that could kill them. Invariably, Christians who have strayed from the truth and refuse to return filter into our churches and spread the cancer of division and strife. Strong leaders must learn to endure it wisely. And just as a surgeon must operate in order to cut out diseased tissue, so leaders in churches must confront those who would infect the body of Christ with discord and factions.

DISCOVERING THE WAY

Every calling has its occupational hazards. This is particularly true of leadership. Leaders walk around with a "Kick Me" sign pinned to their backs. So if a leader is to be effective, he or she must cultivate two qualities at the same time. First, the leader must cultivate a tender heart. People aren't to be herded or driven but led. This is especially true of God's people. But this type of leadership takes a tender heart. Without it callousness will replace compassion. The second quality is equally important: a tough hide. A leader will become easily discouraged, perhaps even disillusioned, if that leader doesn't protect his or her heart from caving in under the pressure of criticism and, on occasion, outright verbal assault. Such a tough-hearted message was certainly needed by Titus as he faced difficult challenges on the island of Crete.

Imagine what life must have been like for Titus and the small band of new believers on the island of Crete. What kinds of criticism might Titus have faced from within the church?

_____

_____

_____

Have you been involved in leadership and received criticism? Describe your leadership role and the criticism you received.

_____

_____

_____

What did you think or feel about the criticism you received? How did you deal with it?

_____

_____

_____

A REALISTIC FACT

While all leaders tend to be targets of criticism, those engaged in ministry, at all levels, become recipients of some of the most vicious attacks. Paul understood this fact and wanted to make sure his young protégé Titus was well prepared for criticism that was sure to come. The easy thing to do is to please people rather than stand on principle. But leadership takes more than compassion; it requires conviction and the ability to confront.

A Brief Scriptural Survey

A few examples, along with some principles, will illustrate the fact that leaders, and particularly godly leaders, are walking pin cushions of criticism. But the following men refused to allow the barbs of critics to penetrate their tough hides and prick their tender hearts.

Let's consider the man who parted the Red Sea and led the children of Israel to the Promised Land — Moses. While leading a ragtag band of nomads around in the wilderness, Moses faced criticism from unlikely sources, his brother and sister. They complained about his wife, and they were jealous of his leadership position (Numbers 12:1–2). Though he was leading with humility (Numbers 12:3), Moses had to face the disappointment of his own family turning against him. Here's a warning: Those choosing to lead may face antagonism from the people they love the most.

As he grew from a little shepherd boy into a giant-killer, David was thrown into the spotlight, and not everyone appreciated the sudden glow. For the next twelve years, King Saul's insecurity, jealousy, and self-centeredness drove him to torment his servant David (1 Samuel 18:6–9). Take heed, because leadership often results in resistance and retribution from those above us.

Nehemiah was charged with rebuilding the Jerusalem wall, yet powerful men questioned his motives (Nehemiah 2:19). So just because God clearly calls you to leadership doesn't mean everyone else will accept your role. It takes a tough hide to stand tall and strong against those who oppose your God-given calling.

And who could forget Job, the man who lost his home, his business, and his children? When his friends came to comfort him, they pointed accusing fingers in his face and blamed his suffering on some secret sin (Job 4:1–9). The lesson? Even friends may seek to dissuade you from what you know is true and right.

The New Testament has its share of thick-skinned leaders. Tender-hearted John was still fending off bullies of the faith toward the end of his life (3 John 9–10). Leadership requires courage and a willingness to wield a club to keep protecting the sheep from wolves.

Even the great apostle Paul was not immune to the critics. Writing just before his death he warned Timothy of two men who had hurt him personally—Demas (2 Timothy 4:10) and Alexander (4:14). One deserted him, and the other opposed him. Here's the principle: Some are lost to your influence and must be turned over to the Lord; He'll take care of them.

At least five groups of critics are identified in this biblical survey. Can you relate? Consider some experiences when you received unfair criticism, and fill in the chart below.

Relationship	Name or Initials	Criticism	Your Response
Family			
Friend(s)			
Boss/ Supervisor			
Peer(s)			
Stranger(s)			

Which criticism stung the most? Explain why.

_____

_____

_____

What is the most effective way you've found to endure non-constructive criticism?

_____

_____

_____

A WISE WARNING

Whether they were on the island of Crete or in the metropolitan city of Rome, Paul expected troublemakers to arise, and he warned every leader in the church to put on a tough hide.

Critics carry two dirty tricks in their bags. First, they disseminate "dissensions."[1] They sow discord and plant poisonous seeds of strife, which blossom into bitter fruit that causes division (Romans 16:17). Dissenters also cause hindrances; they "bring about temptations (to sin)."[2] They scandalize leaders. Setting snares, they destroy trust, stir up rumors, and actively seek to topple God's chosen men and women in spiritual leadership. Tragically, churches split, small groups splinter, and God's kingdom suffers by those who are "slaves . . . of their own appetites" (16:18).

A SPECIFIC EXAMPLE

Paul knew Titus wouldn't be immune from such rabble-rousers. So to prepare Titus to handle his critics, Paul gave him three clear instructions about what to say, what to avoid, and whom to reject. Each of these instructions would require a tender heart wrapped in a tough hide.

 Read Titus 3:8.

What to say. As we noted in the previous lesson, Paul commanded Titus "to speak confidently" (Titus 3:8), pushing him to boldly charge believers to unfurl the flag of faith by engaging in good deeds. A life devoted to selfless deeds would silence critics and dissuade the dissenters because they wouldn't find ready ears among those who believe right and behave right.

 Read Titus 3:9.

What to avoid. A leader with a tough hide avoids certain things: "foolish controversies," or theological speculations that can't be supported by God's Word, and getting involved in the unimportant minutia of religion. This would include creating endless "genealogies" not found in the Scriptures and also arguments about the Bible that are only intended to cause "strife and disputes" (Titus 3:9). Critics love to lay these snares along a leader's path because it is easy for him or her to fall into these holes. Once the leader is trapped, dissensions and scandals are sure to follow. That's why Paul warned Titus to avoid such "unprofitable and worthless" chatter.

In contrast to good deeds, which are "good and profitable" (3:8), the "foolish, stupid" [3] talk of critics may appear interesting and even intellectual but ultimately is silly, futile, and pointless.

 Read Titus 3:10–11.

Whom to reject. Unfortunately, there comes a time when leadership requires tough action. Paul impressed upon Titus the necessity of removing a "factious man [or woman]" from the church (Titus 3:10). This is a person whose strong and self-chosen opinions stir up divisions. It would include those who are divisive, disruptive, or destructive to the church. However, God always starts with grace. Paul appealed to Titus to warn the factious person once. If he or she refused to stop rebelling, Titus was to confront the person again. After a second warning, if such a person refused to repent, Titus would have to reject him or her. Sound harsh? Paul said that these people are "perverted," living in sin, and as such, they are "self-condemned" (3:11). The words of William Hendriksen are helpful in understanding what this means.

> Such a person is not living and seeing *straight*. He is *mentally and morally turned or twisted*. . . . He is actually living in sin. What makes his sin very bad is the fact that *he knows* that he is sinning. If his conscience has not already spoken plainly, he has at least been warned, and that not once but twice. Hence, he sins "being self-condemned." [4]

Though grace can and must be extended, critics must not be allowed free reign. There comes a time when they must be silenced, and if they refuse, they must be rejected.

Read Matthew 7:1–5; Matthew 18:15–17; and Ephesians 4:14–16. Why do you think it is so important that a leader maintain a tender heart as well as a tough hide when doing the hard work of speaking truth, avoiding gossip, and confronting and rejecting? What are some possible consequences of neglecting this balance?

_____

_____

_____

_____

Consider what you know about the life and leadership of Jesus. What examples from his life demonstrate a tender heart? How about a tough hide?

_____

_____

_____

STARTING YOUR JOURNEY

Dealing with critics is part of any leader's job description. The best leaders handle their critics with a tender heart and a tough hide—two qualities not easily acquired. Three principles stand out that should help us cultivate these characteristics.

- First, *we must confidently trust that God will ultimately take care of our critics, so we must speak the truth regardless of who takes offense.*

- Second, *we must sadly concede that critics love fruitless controversy, so we must discipline our minds and time to avoid such foolishness.*

- Third, *we must resign ourselves to the fact that critics must sometimes be confronted, so we must face them with grace and justice.*

Take a moment to examine yourself honestly. How tender is your heart, and how tough is your hide? (You may wish to ask a trusted friend or your spouse for a more objective opinion.)

	Like Mush		Soft but Firm		Rigid
Heart	1	2	3	4	5
Hide	1	2	3	4	5

If your heart or hide is too soft, you'll wither under criticism or fail to speak up for truth. If your hide or your heart is too hard, you'll be so callous you'll feel nothing at all or you will end up exercising judgment without grace. What do you personally need to do to find a balance?

_____

_____

_____

The only way we can find the proper balance is to be changed from the inside out. That's not something we can do on our own. Write a prayer below, humbly asking God to shape you into the leader He wants you to be.

_____

_____

_____

_____

Is there a circumstance you're facing right now in which you need to step up and *speak truth*, *avoid foolish talk*, or *reject a dissenter*? If so, write down what you believe the Lord is leading you to do.

_____

_____

_____

❧

J. Oswald Sanders wrote in his definitive work, *Spiritual Leadership*:

> No one need aspire to leadership in the work of God who is not prepared to pay a price greater than his contemporaries and colleagues are willing to pay. True leadership always exacts a heavy toll . . . and the more effective the leadership is, the higher the price to be paid.[5]

A leader never aspires to hear criticism, endure personal attacks, and discipline divisive personalities. But Paul told Titus that it's part of the job description. And what was true then is just as true today. So wrap your tender heart inside a tough hide.

WHEN DOING WHAT'S HARD IS BEST

1 Timothy 5:20–21; Titus 3:10–11

THE HEART OF THE MATTER

God's work is sacred. So when a person engaged in ministry repeatedly defies God's high and holy standards, that individual is "perverted" and is to be removed. Paul's judgment and command are uncompromising. The very reason God's work is holy is because He is holy. Those who minister will never do so without some failures, because they are not holy as He is. God's grace, however, is sufficient to forgive those frailties. But those who cover up a lifestyle of sin behind the façade of sacred ministry must be confronted and removed.

DISCOVERING THE WAY

The consequence of violating God's sacred work, that which is performed for God's glory and the church's edification, is severe—disqualification from ministry—because His work bears His mark and reflects His reputation. Because this is true, God sets the boundaries in which His work is to be accomplished. The standards are high and holy. That is why Paul warned Timothy and Titus to treat with care any accusations against those who minister but not to falter when confrontation was necessary.

Most of us have had conversations with someone in which we had to confront that person for his or her behavior. Think of one such time in your life, and briefly describe the situation.

_____

_____

_____

_____

What steps did you take to ensure you had the correct facts before you confronted the person?

_____

_____

_____

How did you actually confront the other person, and what was the result?

_____

_____

_____

_____

From Tabernacle to Temple to Hearts

Since the creation of humankind, God has been at work in the lives of His people. In His infinite creativity, God has varied the method by which His sacred work has been performed, but His standard has never changed: He requires holiness from those who serve Him.

After the Lord led Israel out of slavery in Egypt and they
wandered in the desert, doing the Lord's work consisted of serving
in the tabernacle, a portable building where the people worshiped.
Priests who served wore sacred garments, did their work around
sacred furniture, read the sacred Scriptures, and carried out sacred
sacrifices for God's sacred purposes (Exodus 39–40). Priests who
failed to maintain the holiness of God's work often paid with their
lives, because God is serious about His work being done His way
(Numbers 3:4; 1 Samuel 2:12–17, 22–25, 34).

Under the reigns of David and Solomon, the place for worshiping
God changed from temporary to permanent with the construction of
the temple in Jerusalem (1 Chronicles 28–29; 2 Chronicles 2–3).
The structure may have changed, but God's standard remained. God's
work continued to be sacred. Over the passing of time, the temple
ultimately was destroyed because God's people compromised His
standards (2 Chronicles 36:14–19).

After a time, and in His mercy and grace, God sent His Son to
earth to die, removing the barrier of sin between God and humans.
After He rose again and before He ascended to heaven, Jesus sent us
His Spirit (John 14:16–19; Ephesians 3:16–17), no longer to inhabit
temples "made by human hands" (Acts 7:48) but ones made by divine
hands. No longer residing in a building, God has moved into the lives
of His people (1 Corinthians 3:16; 6:19). We who are believers form
"the church of the living God" (1 Timothy 3:15). From tabernacle to
temple to hearts—God's standard for holiness has never changed. It's
just more personal now.

**The context of 1 Corinthians 3:16–17 refers to the Corinthian
church as God's "temple"—the place where His Spirit dwells and
sacred work is performed. The one who would destroy the temple
is anyone who would divide the church. Think about your local
church. How sacred do you consider the work performed there?**

Common		A Mixed Bag		High and Holy
1	2	3	4	5

Why did you evaluate the sacredness of the work at your church the way you did?

_____

_____

_____

How sacred do you think God considers the work performed in your local church, and why?

Common		A Mixed Bag		High and Holy
1	2	3	4	5

_____

_____

_____

Because sacred work must begin with clean hearts and hands, Paul shifted the metaphor of the temple from the church to the individual. In 1 Corinthians 6:19, what is the temple of God?

_____

_____

What does Paul say we should do to keep the temple clean? (1 Corinthians 6:17, 20)

_____

_____

WHEN A LEADER IS ACCUSED

Paul's admonitions in 1 Corinthians apply to all Christians, but they are to be of particular concern to Christian leaders. For both the layperson and the leader, God offers forgiveness. But for the leader who harms his or her body as well as the church, there is also judgment.

As we will discuss later, Paul instructed Titus to deal with leaders drawn into the sin of factious strife and disputes. But first we will read about how Paul instructed another young protégé, Timothy, how to handle sinful leaders.

 Read 1 Timothy 5:19–22.

At times in the life of a church, an accusation comes against one of its spiritual leaders. So Paul instructed Timothy to tune out hearsay and turn a deaf ear to gossip or suspicious hunches rather than act quickly on every rumor. Setting the bar high, Timothy was to receive only hard evidence, accompanied by provable and viable facts, presented by "two or three witnesses" (1 Timothy 5:19).

The offense, once verified, was not to be ignored, not secretly addressed, not overlooked, and not swept under the rug. Rather, the offender was to be rebuked "in the presence of all" (5:20). The reason was clear—"that the rest also will be fearful of sinning." Since Paul was addressing leadership issues, most likely the "all" represents all who are affected by the offender's leadership: all who have a need to know and all whose lives are directly impacted by the leader being accused. As information is shared openly, an appropriate fear will sweep over the people of God. If someone in the congregation is engaged in the same or similar sin, his or her heart will feel the sting of conviction.

Paul took seriously the sacredness of God's work. That's why he impressed upon Timothy the need to maintain God's standard of holiness. "I solemnly charge you," Paul wrote Timothy (5:21). As one swearing an oath in court, Paul charged Timothy "in the presence of God and of Christ Jesus and of His chosen angels" to preserve the holy work of God within the temple, the church. And he said the principles of investigating and rebuking a sinning leader must never be carried out with "bias" or "partiality," regardless of whom the accused was. He stressed that *any* leader who decides to lead a double life—one of sacredness in public but sinfulness in private—was to be rebuked.

Engaging in God's work is serious because it is sacred business. Therefore, Paul instructed Timothy to be cautious in laying his hands on anyone to commission them for holy service (1 Timothy 5:22).

Have you known a church leader who has been accused of leading a double life? If so, what did the church do?

_____

_____

_____

_____

_____

Based on what we've studied thus far in 1 Timothy 5:19–22, do you think the church handled this situation appropriately? Why, or why not?

_____

_____

_____

_____

If, in your opinion, the church handled the situation inappropriately, what advice could you give the church leaders based on 1 Timothy 5:19–22?

_____

_____

_____

_____

When a Leader Falls

Paul instructed Timothy on the rebuke of a sinning leader. But what if that leader continues in his or her sin—continues to cover the stench of it under the perfume of sacredness? And, as was the case in Crete, what if his or her sin is causing factions in the church? What then?

 Read Titus 3:10–11.

Paul was succinct and brutally clear: such a divisive person is to be rejected (Titus 3:10)! The word Paul used, *paraiteomai*, carried with it the stern action of "discharging" or "dismissing" someone. Or stronger still, to "drive [them] out."[1] Why such drastic action? If the person causing division, dissension, and unrest in the church is allowed to continue, his or her actions could destroy the church, the temple of God (1 Corinthians 3:17). This counsel is especially applicable to leadership in the local church, but it can also apply to any ministry. The sacredness of God's work is not confined to the church's four walls but extends to parachurch ministries, missions organizations, and scores of other ministries.

The text tells us Titus was not to reject an accused leader without careful investigation. Just like Timothy, he was to take pains to confirm that the information was correct and warn the sinning leader, not once but twice, before taking action (Titus 3:10). If the one caught in sin didn't heed the warnings, only then was he or she to be rejected.

Why would such a person reject the opportunity to repent when grace is twice extended? Paul said it is because a divisive person is "warped and sinful" (Titus 3:11 NIV) or "perverted" (NASB). The word *ekstrepho* means to "turn aside,"[2] to be twisted and bent out of shape. A perverted person can't walk a straight line, like a drunkard stumbling in the darkness. He or she is in a sinning state, willfully choosing to violate God's standard of holiness. As such, the individual has already condemned himself or herself.

Perhaps nothing has more potential to blight the sacred work of God than willful, deliberate, and repeated sinfulness by those engaged in ministry. That is why Paul was so pointed in his instruction—"Reject a factious man . . . [because he] is perverted" (3:10–11).

Read Deuteronomy 32:20. What does God say a perverse person lacks? What are some possible results of attempting to minister to God's people without this quality?

What will God do in regard to the "perverse generation" (32:20)? Is there an implication in God's action applicable to us today? Explain.

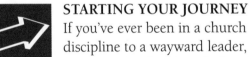

STARTING YOUR JOURNEY

If you've ever been in a church that has had to apply discipline to a wayward leader, you know the sadness and pain associated with "rebuking" and "rejecting" a beloved minister. If you've been part of a church that should have disciplined a sinning leader but didn't, you know the frustration and anger of seeing God's sacred work stained. If you've been a member of a church that has never had a "warped and sinful" leader, you are most fortunate. Regardless of your past experience, you or your church leaders may eventually be faced with doing the hard thing of confronting a sinning minister. If and when that day comes, here are five practical and proven principles to follow.

First, *we must have accurate information based on facts.* If we are committed to maintaining the integrity of God's ministry, we must be willing to do the hard thing. This requires the ability to discern and to listen only to hard facts—not hearsay, rumor, or innuendo.

Second, *we must undertake discipline only when it would be for the overall good of the ministry and be to the benefit of the individual.* The sting from a ministry leader's sin may prick our hearts, but our discipline must never be a personal attack. We must understand that sometimes removal is necessary for the sake of the church and for the purging of the sin in the individual's life.

Third, *we must discipline in a spirit of genuine love and care for the person.* We must also keep in mind that the fallen leader is loved by the Lord and our call is to love him or her as Christ does. We don't uphold the sacredness of God's work if we don't discipline God's way—in grace.

Fourth, *we must carry out the action only after much prayer.* In our zeal for truth, we may be tempted to simply cut off the sinning leader, but we must submit to the wisdom of the Spirit. We must approach the situation with integrity, discernment, and humility.

Finally, *we must have as our goal the restoration of the individual.* Discipline should never condemn but should seek complete repentance and reconciliation of the individual.

Once a leader's sin has been exposed and the leader removed from his or her position, how should the church body treat the former leader? What Scripture(s) can you find to support your answer?

_____

_____

_____

_____

_____

There are times when doing the hard thing is, in fact, the best thing. This is especially true when it comes to God's sacred work. He has always held an extremely high standard for those who handle His Word and who work with His people. James, the brother of Jesus, understood the high and holy work of a minister. That's why he warned: "Let not many of you become teachers, my brethren, knowing that as such we will incur a stricter judgment" (James 3:1). For the leader refusing to repent of his or her sin, part of that "stricter judgment" involves consequences of rebuke and rejection. Though no one relishes administering such judgment, God's work is too important to avoid the hard thing of confrontation when it really is the best thing for the church and the sinning leader.

COVERING ALL THE FINAL BASES

Titus 3:12 – 15

THE HEART OF THE MATTER

When Paul closed his letters, he commonly mentioned various people and situations as if running through a mental checklist. People he hadn't mentioned before, he named. Situations he hadn't addressed, he covered. It's as if he were summing up by naming those individuals he loved and those issues he considered most important, wrapping them into one final bundle. That is exactly what Paul did in his letter to Titus. From this message we can conclude that the difficulties of life are easier to bear with friends at our side and with an attitude of encouragement and grace.

DISCOVERING THE WAY

Confident in his writings and zealous in his actions, Paul was a passionate and firm man, a veteran soldier of the cross with plenty of battle scars. Such people tend to stand aloof and alone. If we read only the openings of Paul's letters, it would be easy to come to the conclusion that he was a lone wolf howling in the wilderness. But even a casual reading of his closing thoughts reveals a much different side of Paul. It's there we meet his friends and hear his burdens. It is with this image of Paul as a burdened friend that we'll close our study of Titus by noting a couple of truths to keep in balance, some priorities to keep in perspective, and a bit of practical advice to keep in mind.

ESSENTIAL TRUTHS TO KEEP IN BALANCE

Before we examine the last four verses of Titus, let's remind ourselves of two essential truths.

First, *God's sacred work usually occurs through people.* Though majestic angels and mighty miracles are a snap away, rarely does the Lord carry out His will on Earth apart from the involvement of His people. For the most part, if a message is to be declared, He uses a human voice. If a message is to be written, He uses human fingers. If a message is to be modeled, He uses a human life. For His own reasons, God picks imperfect people to accomplish a perfect plan.

Think of one specific time when a troubled friend came to you for help. How did God use you to help him or her?

_____

_____

_____

The following verses provide examples of people God chose to participate in His plan. What do these passages tell you about God's timing and the kinds of people He uses to carry out His work?

Jeremiah 1:4–5

_____

_____

Acts 9:10–15

_____

_____

_____

Although God is pleased to use people, He never consults them on the particulars of His plan. This leads to our second truth to keep in balance: *God's sacred plan is unfolding, often in spite of people.* Though He uses people to advance His will, He never stops to ask permission for His direction or purposes.

How would you paraphrase the following passages of Scripture? What does each tell you about God's sovereignty?

Psalm 115:3

_____

_____

Daniel 4:35

_____

_____

FINAL PRIORITIES TO KEEP IN PERSPECTIVE

In keeping with his tradition, Paul concluded his letter to Titus by naming specific people who carried out the sacred work of God. Though they mean little to us today, they meant a great deal to Paul. The evidence we've seen of the highly rational mind of Paul in Titus 1:1–3 gives way to his highly relational heart in 3:12–15. Suddenly, we see the "other side" of Paul, and in doing so, we discover four key priorities.

 Read Titus 3:12.

The first priority, *being together*, is introduced by Paul's naming of two relatively unknown men: Artemas and Tychicus. Nothing is known of Artemas besides his name. His pedigree, credentials, and talents are buried in antiquity. Like a meteor in the night sky, Artemas appeared and vanished, while Tychicus flashes across the biblical sky a few more times (Acts 20:4; Ephesians 6:21; Colossians 4:7; 2 Timothy 4:12) as a trusted envoy and faithful partner of Paul.

Paul planned to send one of these men to Crete to relieve Titus so Titus could travel to Nicopolis and be with Paul. It's assumed that Paul sent Artemas to Crete because Tychicus appears to take over for Timothy in Ephesus (2 Timothy 4:12). When Artemas arrived in Crete, Titus was to "make every effort" to get to Nicopolis. Paul's words reveal a sense of urgency. Though Paul's faith was strong, he needed Titus close.

 DOORWAY TO HISTORY
A Change in Plans: From the Mediterranean
to the Mamertine

We note in Titus 3:12 that Paul planned to spend the winter in the Adriatic resort town of Nicopolis. But more than likely, he never made it (or if he did he didn't spend much time there). We don't know exactly where Paul was when he wrote to Titus, telling him to "make every effort" to come to him, but we know he wasn't in prison. Later he used the exact same words when pleading for Timothy to come to him before winter (2 Timothy 4:21). By that time, Paul had been thrown into the Mamertine dungeon in Rome.[1] Though he longed for the companionship of Titus and Timothy, Paul may not have seen their faces again. He may not have seen the winter, for according to tradition he was beheaded by an official of Nero on the Ostian Road outside of Rome shortly after he sent his second letter to Timothy.[2]

Paul's point is clear: We long to be with others when times are hard. Their presence takes the sting out of loneliness.

Describe the darkest time in your life.

_____

_____

_____

_____

Did you have a friend with you during that time? If so, how did his or her presence help you? If not, what emotions and thoughts did you experience?

_____

_____

_____

_____

 Read Titus 3:13.

The second priority Paul emphasized to Titus besides *being together* was *helping others*. Paul showed that God's sacred work is performed through people by naming two other associates: Zenas the lawyer (like Artemas, his name appears only here), and Apollos, the polished preacher (Acts 18:24–28). They were chosen by Paul to carry the letter to Titus on their way to other ministry assignments.

Paul commanded Titus to "diligently help" them as they passed through Crete. Interestingly, the word for "diligently," *spoudiaos*, is the same word Paul used in Titus 3:12 when he implored Titus to "make every effort," *spoudazo*.[3] Paul's sense of urgency was clear. Titus was to make sure every need of Zenas and Apollos was taken care of by the Cretan congregations. Nothing was to be left undone if it could help these two men in their ministry.

Quite simply, Paul understood the truth that life is enriched by helping others.

When you have a need that you can't meet, what is your typical emotional response? What action do you typically take? Circle your answers below.

	Panic				Pray
Reaction	1	2	3	4	5
	Isolation				Ask for Help
Action	1	2	3	4	5

Explain your answers, especially if your reaction is the opposite of your action.

_____

_____

_____

How has your life been enriched by allowing others to meet your needs? Even though you know this, why can asking for help sometimes be so hard?

_____

_____

_____

 Read Titus 3:14.

Paul urged Titus to be engaged in being together and to keep helping others. And Titus also had an opportunity to teach his congregations the third priority: *doing good.*

Three important observations can be found in these verses about doing good works. First, it's not natural; it's a learned trait. Titus's example of doing good to Zenas and Apollos would serve as a living model for his congregations to "engage in good deeds." Second, Paul instructed Titus to teach his people how to take care of "pressing needs." Needs aren't always announced, so sensitivity is required. Titus was to lead the way. Third, Titus was to encourage his people that meeting needs will be rewarded by the Lord—"they will not be unfruitful."

Too often we fail to meet needs or remain insensitive to others' needs because we are too busy living our own lives or are too reticent, not wanting to embarrass anyone or ourselves. But when this happens, we miss out on God's blessings. What does each verse promise?

Matthew 10:42

_____

_____

Matthew 25:34

_____

_____

Hebrews 6:10

_____

_____

 Read Titus 3:15.

The fourth all-important priority was first established by Paul at the beginning of his letter (Titus 1:4) and is now revisited at the end: *spreading grace*. It's a thoughtful reminder that we aren't alone.

To a man on a lonely ministry outpost, far from the applause of his friends and supporters, Paul sent cheers across the sea: "All who are with me greet you." Titus wasn't forgotten, nor were those in his congregation. Paul sent his hello to "those who love us in the faith," saying, "Grace be with you all" (3:15). Grace was Paul's hallmark. And although he couldn't be with Titus, his faithful friend, he could still pass along God's grace to him—and to all on Crete who loved the Lord.

What makes the message of grace an encouragement and a comfort during trying times, according to these passages?

2 Corinthians 12:9–10

_____

_____

_____

1 Peter 1:13

_____

_____

_____

STARTING YOUR JOURNEY

The picture of this tough-minded apostle is made complete by reading his tenderhearted greetings of grace. Paul understood the burdens life brings. He also knew that burdens aren't as heavy when friends extend the ministry of encouragement and grace by shouldering some of the weight.

Life is hard to bear sometimes, but with friends it is bearable. This is particularly true if we extend grace to all by keeping some practical advice in mind. First, _don't let challenges, either in your life or another's life, drive you away. Stay close._ Second, _don't discount the value of the unknowns—those men and women we know little about, but whom God is using in ministry. Encourage someone._

When you are burdened with something, with whom do you share it? Why this person/these people? What God-given qualities make your choice ideal to help you carry your load?

_____

_____

_____

When the challenges of life become overwhelming, many people retreat and withdraw from others. Is this true of you right now? If yes, why do you think you're pulling away? Is this true of a friend? If yes, why do you think your friend is pulling away from you?

_____

_____

_____

What effects do withdrawal and isolation have on the current difficulty? Explain.

_____

_____

_____

What kind of support do you need most from a friend right now? If a friend were invited to shoulder some of your current burdens or encourage you with the message of grace, what changes might occur?

_____

_____

_____

We meet people every day who have needs. Name two people you know who are in need—physically, emotionally, or spiritually. Have you prayed about how God would like to use you to meet that need?

_____

_____

What have you done to meet the need of each person listed above? If you haven't done anything to meet his or her need, what has prevented you—your schedule, your reluctance, or something else?

_____

_____

_____

❧

These few verses at the close of a short letter reveal the humanity of Paul. We see a man balancing essential priorities as he carried on the sacred work of God. If the great apostle cherished the importance of being together with those he loved in the faith, helping others, doing good, and spreading grace, should we not endeavor to "join in following [Paul's] example" (Philippians 3:17) and do the same?

How to Begin a
Relationship with God

Throughout the book of Titus, we can see that this epistle is woven together with the twin threads of grace and godliness. As hard as we try to knit godliness into our lives, without the thread of grace to bind it to our character it simply comes unraveled. Paul and Titus understood this truth. Both men knew God's grace and were known for their personal integrity. Simply put, it was their relationship with God, through His grace, that allowed them to act in godly ways.

The grace Titus knew and experienced in his life was the grace he preached to the Cretans. And that same grace, as the rest of the Bible says, is what we need if we are to begin a vital relationship with God. The Bible marks the path to God with four essential truths. Let's look at each marker in detail.

Our Spiritual Condition: Totally Depraved

The first truth is rather personal. One look in the mirror of Scripture, and our human condition becomes painfully clear:

> There is none righteous, not even one;
> There is none who understands,
> There is none who seeks for God;
> All have turned aside, together they have become
>   useless;
> There is none who does good,
> There is not even one. (Romans 3:10–12)

We are all sinners through and through—totally depraved. Now, that doesn't mean we've committed every atrocity known to human-kind. We're not as *bad* as we can be, just as *bad off* as we can be. Sin colors all our thoughts, motives, words, and actions.

You still don't believe it? Look around. Everything around us bears the smudge marks of our sinful nature. Despite our best efforts to create a perfect world, crime statistics continue to soar, divorce rates keep climbing, and families keep crumbling.

Something has gone terribly wrong in our society and in ourselves—something deadly. Contrary to how the world would repackage it, "me-first" living doesn't equal rugged individuality and freedom; it equals death. As Paul said in his letter to the Romans, "The wages of sin is death" (Romans 6:23)—our spiritual and physical death that comes from God's righteous judgment of our sin, along with all of the emotional and practical effects of this separation that we experience on a daily basis. This brings us to the second marker: God's character.

GOD'S CHARACTER: INFINITELY HOLY

How can God judge each of us for a sinful state we were born into? Our total depravity is only half the answer. The other half is God's infinite holiness.

The fact that we know things are not as they should be points us to a standard of goodness beyond ourselves. Our sense of injustice in life on this side of eternity implies a perfect standard of justice beyond our reality. That standard and source is God Himself. And God's standard of holiness contrasts starkly with our sinful condition.

Scripture says that "God is Light, and in Him there is no darkness at all" (1 John 1:5). God is absolutely holy—which creates a problem for us. If He is so pure, how can we who are so impure relate to Him?

Perhaps we could try being better people, try to tilt the balance in favor of our good deeds, or seek out methods for self-improvement. Throughout history, people have attempted to live up to God's standard by keeping the Ten Commandments or living by their own code of ethics. Unfortunately, no one can come close to satisfying the demands of God's law. Romans 3:20 says, "By the works of the Law no flesh will be justified in His sight; for through the Law comes the knowledge of sin."

OUR NEED: A SUBSTITUTE

So here we are, sinners by nature and sinners by choice, trying to pull ourselves up by our own bootstraps to attain a relationship with our holy Creator. But every time we try, we fall flat on our faces. We can't live a good enough life to make up for our sin, because God's standard isn't "good enough"—it's *perfection*. And we can't make amends for the offense our sin has created without dying for it.

Who can get us out of this mess?

If someone could live perfectly, honoring God's law, and would bear sin's death penalty for us—in our place—then we would be saved from our predicament. But is there such a person? Thankfully, yes!

Meet your substitute—*Jesus Christ*. He is the One who took death's place for you!

> [God] made [Jesus Christ] who knew no sin to be sin
> on our behalf, so that we might become the righteous-
> ness of God in Him. (2 Corinthians 5:21)

GOD'S PROVISION: A SAVIOR

God rescued us by sending His Son, Jesus, to die on the cross for our sins (1 John 4:9–10). Jesus was fully human and fully divine (John 1:1, 18), a truth that ensures His understanding of our weaknesses, His power to forgive, and His ability to bridge the gap between God and us (Romans 5:6–11). In short, we are "justified as a gift by His grace through the redemption which is in Christ Jesus" (Romans 3:24). Two words in this verse bear further explanation: *justified* and *redemption*.

Justification is God's act of mercy, in which He declares believing sinners righteous while they are still in their sinning state. Justification doesn't mean that God *makes* us righteous, so that we never sin again, rather that He *declares* us righteous—much like a judge pardons a guilty criminal. Because Jesus took our sin upon Himself and suffered our judgment on the cross, God forgives our debt and proclaims us PARDONED.

Redemption is God's act of paying the ransom price to release us from our bondage to sin. Held hostage by Satan, we were shackled by the iron chains of sin and death. Like a loving parent whose child has been kidnapped, God willingly paid the ransom for you. And what a price He paid! He gave His only Son to bear our sins—past, present, and future. Jesus's death and resurrection broke our chains and set us free to become children of God (Romans 6:16–18, 22; Galatians 4:4–7).

Placing Your Faith in Christ

These four truths describe how God has provided a way to Himself through Jesus Christ. Because the price has been paid in full by God, we must respond to His free gift of eternal life in total faith and confidence in Him to save us. We must step forward into the relationship with God that He has prepared for us—not by doing good works or by being good people, but by coming to Him just as we are and accepting His justification and redemption by faith.

> For by grace you have been saved through faith; and
> that not of yourselves, it is the gift of God; not as a
> result of works, so that no one may boast.
> (Ephesians 2:8–9)

We accept God's gift of salvation simply by placing our faith in Christ alone for the forgiveness of our sins. Would you like to enter into a relationship with your Creator by trusting in Christ as your Savior? If so, here's a simple prayer you can use to express your faith:

Dear God,

I know that my sin has put a barrier between You and me. Thank You for sending Your Son, Jesus, to die in my place. I trust in Jesus alone to forgive my sins, and I accept His gift of eternal life. I ask Jesus to be my personal Savior and the Lord of my life. Thank You.

In Jesus's name, amen.

If you've prayed this prayer or one like it and you wish to find out more about knowing God and His plan for you in the Bible, contact us at Insight for Living.

Pastoral Ministries Department
Insight for Living
Post Office Box 269000
Plano, Texas 75026-9000
USA
972-473-5097 (Monday through Friday, 8:00 a.m.–
5:00 p.m. Central time)
www.insight.org/contactapastor

ENDNOTES

Unless otherwise noted below, all material in this Bible Companion is adapted from *Tough Grace in Difficult Places: A Study of the Book of Titus* sermon series by Charles R. Swindoll and was supplemented by the Creative Ministries department of Insight for Living.

LESSON ONE

1. Abraham Lincoln telegram to Ulysses S. Grant, April 7, 1865, in *Collected Works of Abraham Lincoln*, ed. Roy P. Basler, vol. 8, electronic ed. (Ann Arbor, Mich.: University of Michigan Digital Library Production Services, 2001), http://name.umdl.umich.edu/lincoln8, accessed December 29, 2006. Also available in print.

2. F. W. Bush, "Crete," in *The International Standard Bible Encyclopedia*, vol. 1, *A–D*, rev. illustrated ed., ed. Geoffrey W. Bromiley and others (Grand Rapids: Eerdmans, 1988), 814.

LESSON TWO

1. R. H. Mounce, "Kerygma," in *The International Standard Bible Encyclopedia*, vol. 3, *K–P*, rev. illustrated ed., ed. Geoffrey W. Bromiley and others (Grand Rapids: Eerdmans, 1987), 9.

LESSON THREE

1. Tom Wright, *Paul for Everyone: The Pastoral Letters 1 and 2 Timothy and Titus*, 2d ed. (Louisville: Westminster John Knox Press, 2004), 143–144.

2. Wright, *Paul for Everyone*, 144.

3. Walter Bauer and others, eds., *A Greek-English Lexicon of the New Testament and Other Early Christian Literature*, 2d rev. ed. (Chicago: University of Chicago Press, 1979), 292.

4. Bauer and others, eds., *A Greek-English Lexicon of the New Testament and Other Early Christian Literature*, 580.

5. Bauer and others, eds., *A Greek-English Lexicon of the New Testament and Other Early Christian Literature*, 808.

Lesson Four

1. C. S. Lewis, *The Weight of Glory: And Other Addresses* (San Francisco: HarperSanFrancisco, 2001), 58.

2. John R. W. Stott, *The Message of 1 Timothy and Titus*, The Bible Speaks Today Series (Downers Grove, Ill.: InterVarsity, 2001), 183.

Lesson Five

1. Walter Bauer and others, eds., *A Greek-English Lexicon of the New Testament and Other Early Christian Literature*, 2d rev. ed. (Chicago: University of Chicago Press, 1979), 832.

2. Bauer and others, eds., *A Greek-English Lexicon of the New Testament and Other Early Christian Literature*, 700.

Lesson Six

1. John R. W. Stott, *The Message of 1 Timothy and Titus*, The Bible Speaks Today Series (Downers Grove, Ill.: InterVarsity, 2001), 189.

2. Walter Bauer and others, eds., *A Greek-English Lexicon of the New Testament and Other Early Christian Literature*, 2d rev. ed. (Chicago: University of Chicago Press, 1979), 829–830.

3. Bauer and others, eds., *A Greek-English Lexicon of the New Testament and Other Early Christian Literature*, 445.

Lesson Seven

1. Walter Bauer and others, eds., *A Greek-English Lexicon of the New Testament and Other Early Christian Literature*, 2d rev. ed. (Chicago: University of Chicago Press, 1979), 304.

2. Bauer and others, eds., *A Greek-English Lexicon of the New Testament and Other Early Christian Literature*, 8.

Lesson Eight

1. Walter Bauer and others, eds., *A Greek-English Lexicon of the New Testament and Other Early Christian Literature*, 2d rev. ed. (Chicago: University of Chicago Press, 1979), 142.

Lesson Nine

1. Walter Bauer and others, eds., *A Greek-English Lexicon of the New Testament and Other Early Christian Literature*, 2d rev. ed. (Chicago: University of Chicago Press, 1979), 200.

2. Bauer and others, eds., *A Greek-English Lexicon of the New Testament and Other Early Christian Literature*, 753.

3. Bauer and others, eds., *A Greek-English Lexicon of the New Testament and Other Early Christian Literature*, 531.

4. William Hendriksen, *Thessalonians, Timothy and Titus: New Testament Commentary* (Ann Arbor, Mich.: Cushing-Malloy, 1981), 396.

5. J. Oswald Sanders, *Spiritual Leadership*, rev. ed. (Chicago: Moody Press, 1980), 169.

Lesson Ten

1. Walter Bauer and others, eds., *A Greek-English Lexicon of the New Testament and Other Early Christian Literature*, 2d rev. ed. (Chicago: University of Chicago Press, 1979), 616.

2. Bauer and others, eds., *A Greek-English Lexicon of the New Testament and Other Early Christian Literature*, 245.

Lesson Eleven

1. J. D. Douglas and Philip W. Comfort, eds., *Who's Who in Christian History* (Wheaton, Ill.: Tyndale House, 1992), 544.

2. Douglas and Comfort, eds., *Who's Who in Christian History*, 545.

3. Walter Bauer and others, eds., *A Greek-English Lexicon of the New Testament and Other Early Christian Literature*, 2d rev. ed. (Chicago: University of Chicago Press, 1979), 763.

Resources for Probing Further

Before you board the ship and sail away from Crete to another adventure in the Bible, allow the truths of the book of Titus to sink in by exploring some of the following suggested resources. Of course, we cannot always endorse everything a writer or ministry says, so we encourage you to approach these and all other non-biblical resources with wisdom and discernment.

Calvin, John. *1 and 2 Timothy and Titus*. The Crossway Classic Commentaries, ed. Alister McGrath and J. I. Packer. Wheaton, Ill.: Crossway Books, 1998.

Fee, Gordon D. *1 and 2 Timothy, Titus*. New International Biblical Commentary—New Testament Series, vol. 13. Peabody, Mass.: Hendrickson, 1988.

Getz, Gene A. *Elders and Leaders: God's Plan for Leading the Church—A Biblical, Historical and Cultural Perspective*. Chicago: Moody Publishers, 2003.

Hughes, R. Kent, and Bryan Chapell. *1 and 2 Timothy and Titus: To Guard the Deposit*. Preaching the Word Series. Wheaton, Ill.: Crossway Books, 2000.

MacArthur, John. *Titus*. The MacArthur New Testament Commentary Series. Chicago: Moody Press, 1996.

Malphurs, Aubrey. *The Dynamics of Church Leadership*. Ministry Dynamics for a New Century Series, ed. Warren W. Wiersbe. Grand Rapids: Baker Books, 1999.

Peterson, Eugene H. *Working the Angles: The Shape of Pastoral Integrity*. Grand Rapids: Eerdmans, 2000.

Phillips, John. *Exploring the Pastoral Epistles: An Expository Commentary*. The John Phillips Commentary Series. Grand Rapids: Kregel, 2004.

Piper, John. *Brothers, We Are Not Professionals: A Plea to Pastors for Radical Ministry*. Nashville: Broadman and Holman, 2002.

Sanders, J. Oswald. *Spiritual Leadership: Principles of Excellence for Every Believer*, 2d revision. Chicago: Moody Publishers, 1994.

Stott, John R. W. *The Message of 1 Timothy and Titus*. The Bible Speaks Today Series. Downers Grove, Ill: InterVarsity, 2001.

Towner, Philip H. *The Letters to Timothy and Titus*. The New International Commentary on the New Testament. Grand Rapids: Eerdmans, 2006.

Wiersbe, Warren W. *Be Faithful (1 and 2 Timothy, Titus, Philemon)*. Colorado Springs: Cook Communications, 1981.

Wright, Tom. *Paul for Everyone: The Pastoral Letters, 1 and 2 Timothy and Titus*. 2d ed. Louisville: Westminster John Knox Press, 2004.

Ordering Information

If you would like to order additional copies of *Tough Grace in Difficult Places: A Study of the Book of Titus Bible Companion* or other Insight for Living resources, please contact the office that serves you.

United States

Insight for Living
Post Office Box 269000
Plano, Texas 75026-9000
USA
1-800-772-8888,
(Monday through Thursday
7:00 a.m. – 9:00 p.m. and
Friday 7:00 a.m. – 7:00 p.m.
Central time)
www.insight.org

Canada

Insight for Living Canada
Post Office Box 2510
Vancouver, BC V6B 3W7
CANADA
1-800-663-7639
www.insightforliving.ca

Australia, New Zealand, and South Pacific

Insight for Living Australia
Post Office Box 1011
Bayswater, VIC 3153
AUSTRALIA
1300 467 444
www.insight.asn.au

United Kingdom and Europe

Insight for Living United Kingdom
Post Office Box 348
Leatherhead
KT22 2DS
UNITED KINGDOM
0800 915 9364
www.insightforliving.org.uk

Other International Locations

International constituents may contact the U.S. office through our Web site (www.insight.org), mail queries, or by calling +1-972-473-5136.